RESTORING the BROKEN WALLS

OF PAST GENERATIONS

ELEANOR BUTKIEWICZ

RESTORING the BROKEN WALLS

OF PAST GENERATIONS

Discovering the Forgotten
Ministry of Jesus Christ

REDEMPTION
PRESS

Re-Published by Redemption Press, PO Box 427, Enumclaw, WA 98022

Toll Free (844) 2REDEEM (273-3336)

This book is designed to provide accurate and authoritative information with regard to the subject matter covered. This information is given with the understanding that neither the author nor Redemption Press is engaged in the rendering legal, professional advice. Since the details of your situation are fact dependent, you should additionally seek the services of a competent professional.

The opinions expressed by the author are not necessarily those of Redemption Press.

Published in the United States of America

ISBN: 978-1-68314-277-5
1. Religion: Christian Ministry: General
2. Religion: Christian Life: Spiritual Warfare

DEDICATION

This book is dedicated to all of God's generals who've gone before me and on whose shoulders I stand—the men and women of God who never wavered from the call of God on their lives, despite the great cost, and who consequently touched their generation with the power and glory of God.

Special thanks to my wonderful Ministry Team—my Army of Warriors—the Green Berets, who've stood shoulder-to-shoulder with me in the trenches and gone behind enemy lines to bring freedom to the captives.

TABLE OF CONTENTS

FOREWARD

The Spirit of the Lord God is upon Me,
Because the Lord has anointed Me
To preach good tidings to the poor;
He has sent Me to heal the brokenhearted,
To proclaim liberty to the captives,
And the opening of the prison to those who are bound;
To proclaim the acceptable year of the Lord,
And the day of vengeance of our God;
To comfort all who mourn,
To console those who mourn in Zion,
to give them beauty for ashes,
The oil of joy for mourning,
The garment of praise for the spirit of heaviness;
That they may be called trees of righteousness,
The planting of the Lord, that He may be glorified.
And they shall rebuild the old ruins,
They shall raise up the former desolations,
And they shall repair the ruined cities,
The desolations of many generations.

Isaiah 61:1–4, NKJV

Foreword (con't)

This scripture is fulfilled every time one of God's people is set free from generational curses and the demons behind those curses are cast out.

Deliverance is all about the opening of the prison to those who are bound, receiving the garment of praise for spirits of heaviness (depression), and making His people trees of righteousness—a holy people—when they no longer have to struggle with spirits of lust and perversion that have come down the bloodline.

It is rebuilding the old ruins from the sins of past generations and the repairing of the ruined "cities," which would be our families that have been made desolate by many generations of ancestral sin in the bloodline. God wants to redeem our bloodlines. In the Book of Nehemiah, we see that Nehemiah was sent back to Jerusalem to repair the walls of the City of Jerusalem. The walls of the city were unrepaired, leaving its people defenseless and vulnerable. Walls were critical in the Old Testament times to protect the inhabitants of the city and to keep invading pagan armies from destroying God's people.

Whenever a demon is cast out of one of God's children, it is the day of vengeance of our God on Satan and his hordes of hell who have "come to kill, steal, and destroy" (John 10:10, NKJV).

Thank you, Holy Spirit, for the revelation of the spirit world. Thank you, Jesus, for putting Satan under our feet by your finished work at the cross! Thank you, Lord, that you said if we believe in you and the things that you do, even *greater* than these things shall we do in your marvelous, matchless name (John 14:12).

It is my hope that as you read this book, you will begin to understand our heavenly Father's great love for us, his creation, and that he is still the God of the miraculous! "Jesus Christ, the same yesterday, today and forever" (Hebrews 13:8, NKJV).

THE FORGOTTEN MINISTRY OF JESUS: DELIVERANCE

"And He was preaching in their synagogues
throughout all Galilee and casting
out demons" (Mark 1:39, NKJV)

Just as God rose up and prepared Moses to deliver his people from Egyptian captivity, so has he sent us a greater deliverer, Jesus Christ. Moses was commanded to go to Pharaoh with this message from God: "Let my people go!" Jesus Christ is saying the same thing to Satan in this day, "Let my people go!"

Jesus Christ came some two thousand years ago to help suffering humanity. He worked miracles, healed the sick, and cast out demons. This never changed throughout his entire three and a half years of ministering to people.

Almost everywhere in the Gospels when Jesus performed a healing miracle, it says, "He cast out demons and healed the sick." They went hand in hand. It seems Jesus never made any distinction between healing people's sicknesses and delivering them from demons. This was characteristic of Jesus's ministry from beginning to end. It was the same with preaching, as shown in the following scripture, "And He was preaching in their synagogues throughout all Galilee, and casting out demons" (Mark 1:39, NKJV).

The focus of Jesus's ministry was primarily to the "lost sheep of the house of Israel," the Jews who attended synagogue every Sabbath. They were normal, respectable, religious people, just like you and I, who had demonic oppression in their lives. They were everyday people who had families and worked to make a living just like millions of Christians today. That's where the similarity stops because He set these people free. Are we doing the same with God's people today?

Didn't Jesus instruct us in the Great Commission to "Go ye into all the world preach the Gospel … cast out demons … " (Mark 16:15–18, NAS)? In the book of Matthew it says, "He called unto him his twelve disciples and gave them authority over unclean spirits to cast them out" (Matthew 10:1 NAS).

Then in the book of Matthew it says, "As you go, preach, saying, the kingdom of heaven is at hand. Heal the sick, raise the dead, cleanse the lepers, cast out demons; freely you received, freely give" (Matthew 10:7–8, NAS).

Yet how many churches do we see today that take that scriptural mandate seriously? We do a great job in teaching the Word, praying to heal the sick, but the casting out of demons is nearly unheard of in the modern day Church.

The first century church is the only church that completely followed the pattern and clear revelation of Jesus's ministry as recorded in the Gospels. Early church records show that as soon as people were saved, they would be taken through deliverance. The intervening centuries show that churches became steeped in religious tradition that has obscured that revelation and pattern of Jesus. As a result, God's people have been left to suffer demonic oppression without the help so desperately needed. I believe it is the day and the hour to re-establish the church once again on the clear pattern established for us by Jesus in the Gospels.

History shows that in the ensuing centuries since Jesus's three and a half years of earthly ministry, there have been people called with miraculous ministries to the sick and afflicted. Sadly enough, nowhere in history is there record of one of God's people having a ministry of casting out demons, which corresponded to the magnitude of Jesus's ministry. Oh, there have been great men of God like Derek Prince and Win Worley, who operated in the area of deliverance, but no one who had a great ministry of deliverance which paralleled the healing ministries of people like Kathryn Kuhlman, Jack Coe, Maria Woodworth Etter, and Benny Hinn. I believe that is about to change in this end time.

Could it be that Satan so opposes deliverance ministry that most people who are called to it stay hidden due to the fierce attacks coming from his headquarters? Many times these attacks come through other well meaning Christians who are steeped in religious doctrine that denies the reality of demons. Satan aims all his big guns at anyone called to this type of ministry, and many times people retreat out of fear and discouragement, not being able to withstand the onslaught. That is changing! God has raised up this woman, as well as others who are solidly grounded in the Word and who have been able to withstand the onslaught of the enemy and press through to the call on their lives, despite the cost! I have had many come to me and say, "I don't even want to know what this anointing has cost you." They're right, it has cost me dearly—a price most would not be willing to pay. I have died ten thousand deaths, but "I press toward the mark for the prize of the high calling of God in Christ Jesus" (Philippians 3:14 KJV).

One of God's generals, Derek Prince, who had a deliverance ministry for thirty years, said that he soon came to realize that Satan has developed a special opposition to the deliverance ministry. He went on to say that because Satan is a creature of darkness, he prefers to keep the true nature of his activities concealed. If he can keep humanity unaware of his tactics, or of his very existence, he can use the twin tools of ignorance and fear to open the way for his destructive purposes.

Satan, being the clever creature that he is, has put so much fear into people on the subject of the demonic through movies like *The Exorcist*, where the demons exhibited such great power and evil and seemed to be stronger than the ones attempting to cast them out. His plot, of course, is to make people afraid of deliverance and to totally avoid the subject. If people sat through a genuine deliverance session at Isaiah 61 Ministries, they would see that it's something that is done with great calm and order.

Isaiah 61 Ministries is the ministry that I founded under the direction of the Holy Spirit. I have a well-trained group of Deliverance Ministers who assist me in breaking bondages and bringing healing to God's people. We are located in Phoenix, Arizona, and we hold meetings twice a month at a church which is listed on our Web site, www.healing-deliverance.com. The meetings are grounded with sound Biblical teaching given by myself and followed by the breaking of strongholds and generational curses that have come down the bloodline, which I explain fully in the chapter on Generational Curses.

The ministry was birthed out of a desperate situation in my life some sixteen years ago when a family member married someone who was heavily demonized, violent, and brought great distress into my life. At that time, I knew nothing about deliverance, but I could see that this woman's problems were not natural, but rather supernatural. So I found a basic book on Spiritual Warfare that, for the first time in my Christian life, opened my eyes to the fact that demons can actually be in a person. I then called all over the country trying to find deliverance for this young woman, all to no avail. I did finally find a couple of women in Phoenix who actually did deliverance, thank God!

From that point on, God began to bring all kinds of people in my life that needed this type of help, so I started to educate myself on the subject by getting every book I could find on the subject of deliverance. The Holy Spirit did the rest! I would pick and choose the things that seemed to make sense and forego what didn't click in my Spirit. Kind of like eating fish—you eat the meat and spit out the bones!

My ministry had its roots in my home as I began to minister to people one by one and saw the miracles that God did in their lives. Some things we just learn by getting in there and rolling up our sleeves and through trial and error. In this type of ministry, one learns a great deal about the spiritual realm, and it is an ongoing learning. It is on the job training. I expanded my ministry by getting like-minded people to assist me, and as I trained them, I soon had a good team of warriors. The need was so great that I couldn't keep up with it. I began to see the multitudes of God's people who'd been suffering needlessly with bondages and torment from abusive childhoods or generational curses. They knew they needed more than what they were receiving through the normal channels of counseling and standing on The Word. I would hear the same thing over and over again, "Where's the abundant life we've been promised?"

I didn't *seek* Deliverance Ministry. I was thrust into it. Never in my wildest imagination would I have dreamt that God would use me to come against the powers of darkness in people's lives! I recently read a comment by Larry Jones who has the Feed The Children organization that has gone across the globe. He said after ten years of incredible growth and finances coming in, he and his wife sat down and asked, "Why would God choose us?"

He said they finally figured it out. It was because they didn't know what they were doing. When you don't know what you're doing, you've got to walk on your knees. That is the story of Isaiah 61 Ministries that has touched people from all around the Globe—the Philippines, Grenada, China, South Africa, London, Canada, Australia and Switzerland, to name a few.

Requirements of a Deliverance Ministry

A vital requirement when a person is called to this type of ministry is living a life of obedience to The Lord and His Word. A holy life is the best protection against demonic attack. I saw many fall by the wayside due to sin in their lives. Our spiritual authority is in direct proportion to spiritual intimacy. Our power comes from the indwelling Holy Spirit. Our authority comes from staying close to Jesus Christ.

The Bible tells us that God is the same yesterday, today, and forever. The same God who parted the Red Sea for His people to go across on dry ground, who fed His people manna from heaven for forty years as they wandered in the desert, who led them by a cloud by day and a pillar of fire at night, is available to His people today. Unfortunately because much of the twenty-first century church has relegated God to a tiny box and because we have not followed the pattern set for us by Jesus, i.e. casting out of demons, we have limited the way that God is allowed to move in our lives. We are not seeing the God of the miraculous—the extraordinary miracles of the New Testament. We have become such an intellectual church that we've completely forgotten the simplicity of the gospel. Paul said, and I paraphrase, "I preach the Gospel, not with wise and persuasive words, but with the demonstration of the *power* of the gospel" (1Corinthians 2:4, NIV). Deliverance is the *power arm* of God.

There is a two-fold purpose for this book. The first is to firmly etch into the reader's heart that God is a loving heavenly Father—a Father whose heart it is to restore mankind to the wholeness He originally intended for us before Adam and Eve sinned in the garden and brought sin and its consequences into this world. He is a God of restoration; that is His very nature. As T.L. Osborn once said, "God is a good God; the devil is a bad devil."

The second is to give the reader the understanding of how Satan and his hordes of hell scheme against us. The enemy then delights when God gets blamed for the bad things that happen in our lives. We will look at sin and its consequences in our lives and how the sin of the generations past is still affecting us today.

God has made provision through Jesus Christ's death on the cross for the restoration of everything Satan and his cohorts from hell have stolen from us—emotionally, physically, spiritually, relationally, and financially. One of the ways He does this is through the ministry of deliverance—the casting out of demons. It was fully one-third of Jesus's ministry when He walked this earth. If the modern day church were following the pattern established for us by Jesus Christ, we too would be casting out demons as a normal part of church life.

If we want to see power restored to the church, we must restore the forgotten ministry of Jesus Christ—the ministry of deliverance, i.e. the casting out of demons. It is my personal belief from the things the Holy Spirit has shown me that the next move of God will be a move of holiness. In order for that to happen it must be preceded by a major cleansing of the body of Christ. In order to be holy, the body needs to be cleaned up from sexual sin, compromise, and addictions. The power of God can only be released into a cleansed and holy vessel.

This next generation is hungry to see the power of God. When they don't see it in the Church, many turn to the occult and Satanism because they see power, albeit dark power, which unbeknownst to them carries a heavy price tag.

I had a sixteen-year-old young man come to one of my deliverance sessions with his parents who are both college professors. He sat through half the session, and when we stopped to take a break he came up to me and told me the following: "I've been raised in the church, and I've never seen anything like this before. It's nice to see something real in the church for the first time, to see God's power on display." I think that statement speaks for the entire younger generation.

Because there is so little understanding about what deliverance really is, there are countless hundreds of thousands of sincere Christians who are turning to the world for help because they're not finding the kind of help they need in the church. So they go to doctors, psychiatrists, and psychologists who then give them the only help they can offer—drugs. They go to doctors, psychiatrists, and psychologists who often medicate them. They prescribe uppers, downers, and antidepressants; they all have physical and mental side effects. Those who are bound up oftentimes end up with even more problems than when they began.

A classic example of this is the case of the Northern Illinois University student who killed five people and then himself in February of 2008. The newspapers didn't say that he was a Christian, but he is representative of what is going on in our nation today. They interviewed his girlfriend afterwards, and she said he was probably the nicest, most caring person she ever knew. She said that he had stopped taking an antidepressant about three weeks prior to the incident because "it made him feel like a zombie." There is a good chance that he had depression because of unresolved childhood issues. Oftentimes in cases like this the individual was abused as a child and never received healing for it; thus the resulting depression, which will then show up in his adult life. It may have been something in his bloodline—a history of depression; and there's the possibility that someone in his bloodline had committed murder and that generational spirit of murder was acting out in him.

There was a similar case of the man named Robert Louis Roberts who was a Christian; he killed his two precious children and then shot himself in November of 2007 in Phoenix, Arizona. The newspaper account stated that he had a family history deeply rooted in suicide, depression, substance abuse, mood disorders, and alcoholism. This is what was operating in him. These things coming through the bloodline are generational curses. When his wife told him she wanted a divorce, he got a gun and threatened suicide. Then he went to his pastor for help, but because his pastor didn't know how to deal with the spiritual roots of his problems, he was sent to a psychiatrist who prescribed an antidepressant. The article also stated that he was a very good father and adored his children.

His death and the death of his children could have been prevented if the unclean spirits in operation would have been recognized and cast out of him. He had spirits of depression, murder, and suicide in operation. I have cast out hundreds of thousands of similar spirits from other Christians and seen them totally set free and their lives turned around completely.

In the February 2008 issue of "Charisma" magazine there was another article about a shooting at Youth With A Mission (YWAM) and New Life Church facilities in Denver and Colorado Springs, Colorado. When twenty-four-year-old gunman Matthew Murray opened fire, YWAM staff members Tiffany Johnson, twenty-six, and Philip Crouse, twenty-four were killed. Twelve hours later he opened fire in the parking lot of New Life Church in Colorado Springs—wounding two, killing teenage sisters Stephanie and Rachel Works, and then killing himself. Murray had been a student at the YWAM

Denver facility in 2002, but the ministry said its program directors stated that "issues with his health" made it inappropriate for him to continue. They said that Murray claimed to hear voices. He was a Christian and was raised in a loving Christian home. His father was a respected physician and his mother a stay-at-home mom.

What a tragedy! If he heard voices in his head, it was demons speaking to him. Many of the people I've ministered to have told me that prior to going through deliverance they'd always heard voices in their heads. If something has a voice, it is a living entity, albeit an invisible living entity.

How many times have we read newspaper accounts of people who've just committed murder saying, "God told me to do it." Those demons love to make the world think that God is a God of evil. Can you just see Satan's hordes rejoicing at that? We, who know the Word of God, know that one of God's Commandments in Exodus 20:13 is "Thou shall not commit murder." Would God go against His own commandment? I hardly think so!

I've heard well-meaning Christian leaders say that fasting will break those strongholds in us. First of all, the word *stronghold* is used so loosely in the church, and most often people don't have the slightest knowledge of what a stronghold is. In fact I just heard a pastor speaker at a church, who has written a book on deliverance; he has billed himself as an expert in calling out a stronghold demon out of a person. Well, there is no such thing as a stronghold demon.

A stronghold is a network of demons that are reinforcing and surrounding an emotional wound. The emotional wounding that took place—usually in childhood—opened the door for a demon to come in, and he has brought all kinds of other demons in with him. For example, a child that has been sexually abused by a father or stepfather has a wound that is an open door for demons. The demons that come in and compound that wound are shame, guilt, self-hate, self-blame, rejection of femininity or masculinity, lust, and promiscuity; promiscuity will usually lie dormant until the teen years and early adulthood.

Does Fasting Break Strongholds?

Fasting in and of itself is not going to take care of these very complex issues. There needs to be inner healing by someone who knows what they're doing, followed by a casting out of all the demons that I listed above. The following case is a classic example of what I am saying:

Many years ago, I ministered to a lady in her mid-forties who needed deliverance ministry desperately, but it had never been talked about or taught in the church. As a little girl, she had been severely abused by her mother. Her mother would wake her up in the middle of the night and start beating her. She took her out in the middle of the desert and tried to run her over. There was so much more that I won't go into.

When this woman reached adulthood, she got saved and became a radical Christian. She still had a lot of demons that entered into her through all that abuse, and she also had multiple personalities. She would go on forty-day fasts where she'd fast all food and only drink water for forty days. She told me that while she'd be fasting, something would pick her up off her bed and throw her against the wall. She didn't understand it. I explained to her that the fasting caused the demons in her to manifest, and they became violent with her.

I then took her through powerful deliverance and inner healing. When I would call up her demons, they would usually make her eyeballs roll backward so that you couldn't even see the pupils, or they would cause her eyes to cross—anything to avoid looking at me. When someone has strong demons that are not cooperating, I command them to look at me because this weakens the demons. When I did that with her demons, they'd scream at me and say, "No, I can't look at you. It's disgusting! I see Him, meaning Christ, in your eyes." Another time when I commanded the demons to look at me, they'd cause her eyes to shut tight. When I again commanded them to open her eyes and look at me, the demon shouted, "I can't look. It's too bright in here. Too many of the holy ones in this room." Well, the room wasn't bright, but the Holy Spirit was there—the spirit of Jesus who is the light of the world! Also the angels of God were the "holy ones" the demon couldn't stand to see. Demons love darkness. They hate the holiness of God's kingdom!

After a series of deliverance and inner healing sessions, this woman who'd been tormented all of her life was finally set free. She'd finally found the kind of help she needed! There are thousands of Christians sitting in our churches with similar backgrounds and similar struggles.

You know, the devil never does anything new. He just repeats the same patterns over and over again. Nine out of ten women who call me have the same story: abusive parents, sexual abuse, alcoholic parents; this breeds adult depression, anxiety attacks, and repetition of what they were raised with. The devil loves to bring childhood traumas and wounds so he can set up his network of demons in the next generation and the next and the next. Someone in that generational line must finally find the "hidden" ministry of Jesus Christ—deliverance—so those patterns will be broken and the demons cast out!

TRUE DELIVERANCE VS. INEFFECTIVE DELIVERANCE

I want to give the reader a clear understanding of what true deliverance ministry is all about. Unfortunately, when deliverance is offered, it is sometimes very ineffective, flaky, or weird; then when people don't get the needed results, deliverance itself is viewed as ineffective. The reality is that many who attempt deliverance simply don't have a full understanding of the ministry of deliverance and the spirit realm. Thus the results are less than desirable. Some people know just enough to be dangerous. Misinformation is worse than no information.

Although the casting out of demons is mostly ignored in the majority of Christian churches, when it is practiced, it is largely ineffective. I've heard some evangelists and preachers say to someone needing deliverance, "Come out, you devil! Satan, you come out of this one," and absolutely nothing happens. They are sent away with this message: "Grab it by faith! You've been delivered. Now stand on it." What a travesty! When the person discovers that they have the same exact oppression and torment as before, they feel condemned, thinking they must not have enough faith. After all, didn't the preacher say, "You've been delivered; now just grab it by faith"? Then the enemy begins to do a number on them, making them think there's something seriously wrong with *them*. In reality, they received absolutely *no* deliverance.

First of all, Satan does not inhabit a human being, as he is a fallen angel and not a demon, which I cover in another chapter. Demons are the only spiritual entities that seek to inhabit human beings. Secondly, there is never one demon in a person. They always work in gangs. They always establish a demonic network in someone. For instance, if a demon of rejection is there, he always brings with him self-rejection, fear of rejection, as well demons of unworthiness and self-hate. Third, they all have names, so to just use a broad command such as, "Come out, you devil," is ignorance gone to seed! The other scenario that can happen is covered in the following paragraphs:

Lessons from Failed Deliverances

Many years ago, I attended a small church where the young pastor had gotten into deliverance. At the end of the service, a very strong demon manifested in a young woman whom I knew to be extremely rebellious. It threw her to the floor, and she spent hours writhing on the floor like a snake, while dozens of people were shouting at the demon to come out. The more people shouted at the demon the more confusion there was. The young woman continued writhing on the floor like a snake, her hands manifesting in a claw-like manner.

Had someone in that group asked the Holy Spirit for a word of knowledge as to the name of the demon that was manifesting or had they gotten into that young woman's face and commanded that demon to tell them its name, it would have been over very quickly. The logic behind that is that like a mad dog that's coming at you, if you know his name, you can stop him dead in his track by saying clearly and firmly, "No, Fido." It is the same with demons. If you know their name, they have to obey, and it saves hours of torment for the person who's manifesting. Getting a name, whether it's a mad dog attacking you or a demon manifesting, gives you the upper hand. In both cases, it gives you a handle in bringing one or both of these into subjection. A little later in this book, we'll study the ways that Jesus ministered deliverance to God's people, and as we look at the various episodes where he cast out demons, we will see that Jesus seemed to have found it necessary to ask a demon, "What is your name?" in order to successfully cast out the demon(s).

Unfortunately no one knew what they were doing, myself included at that time. Therefore the show went on for three long hours, wearing everyone out. But the demon was enjoying it!

The other factor involved is that demons are legalists. They know the laws that God set into the universe, and they have to abide by those laws. Unconfessed sin is a legal right for demons to be in a person, as is unforgiveness. So if you're trying to cast a demon out without taking them through renunciation of their sins and also taking them through forgiveness of the people in their lives who have hurt them, the demon will have a legal right to stay. There's also the fact that many times the demon is attached to unhealed childhood wounds. Therefore, if these are not taken care of, the demon may leave temporarily if he's harassed enough, but he will return as soon as the person leaves the place, knowing he has a legal right to be there.

To add to the confusion of this situation was the fact that everyone was yelling something different at this demon making the demons as confused as those doing the "deliverance." Think of it this way, if five different people are shouting different commands at a dog, whose command is he going to obey? Probably nobody's! All that's going to happen is that he's going to get confused and go into a frenzy, which is what happened in this church. While the people meant well, the deliverance did nothing more than torment and humiliate the young woman who left just as bound up as when she came. Ignorance is not bliss!

In much of the body of Christ, the ministry of deliverance is frowned upon simply because there's been a lot of flakiness and weirdness associated with it, as I said before. The reality is there is nothing weird or flaky about true deliverance. In fact, it is highly organized, methodical, and really quite simple.

Emergency Deliverance

Years ago, after I had just started my deliverance ministry in a Phoenix area church, one Sunday evening there was an altar call and a group of people went forward. The eighteen-year-old son of a church family also went forward, and I noticed an overwhelming smell of alcohol on him. When he got under the anointing, a demon manifested in him, and he was thrown to the floor. Immediately the pastor ordered five or six of the men in the church to try and get this demon taken care of. They had to pin him to the floor, and it took all six of the men to hold him down, as the demon was so violent. They all began to shout at the demon, and the more they shouted at him, the more violent it became.

As I was standing there watching, the young man's mother, knowing I had a deliverance ministry, asked me to help. I made my way in there and got on my knees next to that young man's face; after seeing that the demon was making him froth at the mouth while his eyes rolled back in his head, I got into his face and said, "What's your name, spirit?" The demon immediately recognized me (you become known in the spirit world when you do deliverance), and said, "You!"

I said, "Yes, me! Now tell me your name, you foul spirit!" He said his name was Death, so I broke the curse of death over this young man and commanded that death spirit to renounce his claim on him, his bloodline, and all future generations. I had him say, "I come out of Charlie, and I now go to the pit!" As soon as he finished what I commanded him to say, I commanded it to come up and out of Charlie and to go to the pit! With that, it came out of him through violent coughing and retching, and the young man was immediately back in his right mind—quite frightened but happy.

We see evidence of three spiritual truths here:

1. Demons know those with authority.

2. When you get their name, they have to obey.

3. When you have them renounce their claim to the person, it weakens them.

I mentioned earlier that casting out demons without having the person renounce sin and taking him through forgiveness is a legal right for demons not to leave. That still holds true. However, there are times when situations arise like the one I just outlined for you when you will not be able to go through those procedures. Then we operate like paramedics when they come upon the scene of an accident and start to minister to the victim. They aren't able to find out that person's history and what types of medications he's allergic to. They just go to work and do everything in their power to save that person's life.

The same truth applies to a strong demon suddenly manifesting and taking the person over. You're just thrust into it, and you can at least get some kind of help to that person by following the three spiritual truths I outlined in the previous paragraph. When you do those three things, the demon has to obey and leave that person, and the person is not left thrashing all over the floor for hours.

You also may be wondering why the unclean spirit in that young man was "death" instead of "rebellion" or "alcoholism." Well, death was there to try and destroy him, most likely through a drunk driving accident, but also through spiritual death, which will come with addictions. The others were there also. Since I knew that demons work in groups and there is never just one demon in a person, I scheduled an appointment for him the next day.

In this particular young man, he had a very emotionally distant father and felt great rejection from him, and rejection always leads to rebellion. Rejection is the root, and rebellion is the fruit. The rebellion then led him to alcoholism, which further opened doors for other demons to come. There were a whole host of demons in this person.

Demonic Manifestations

When the anointing is strong, demons manifest. That is why you see such bizarre things going on in places like the Toronto Outpouring. When I read that people were barking like dogs and crowing like roosters under the anointing, I knew that it was demons manifesting, not the Holy Spirit. The Holy Spirit is a gentleman and would certainly not manifest as a dog or a rooster. These were probably animals that their ancestors worshipped or used in some sort of occult ritual, thus those spirits came down the bloodline, having never been cast out.

Derek Prince, whom I mentioned earlier, said that when he was in Zambia holding a group deliverance what he saw was astounding. He saw animal spirits begin to manifest in this entire group of people. He said there was a cacophony of jungle sounds. Someone with a lion spirit attempted to charge him, others dug in the ground with their noses like boars. A number of women slithered on their bellies on the ground like snakes. He said that the Africans in that area were keen hunters of animals and had been taught by witch doctors that, in order to be successful, they must open themselves up to the spirit of the particular animal, such as a lion, elephant, or boar that they intended to hunt. When he began the deliverance session, all those animal spirits started to manifest.

Africans are not the only ones who opened themselves up to animal spirits. There was much witchcraft done in the European forests with animals. I have also had many of Latin American descent tell me that as children they were taken into the woods, and their parents subjected them to witchcraft rituals of roosters being slaughtered and the blood put upon them to supposedly ward off evil spirits and bring success into the child's life.

There are sometimes subtle differences between Holy Spirit manifestations and demonic manifestations. It takes great discernment to differentiate. Many times I have seen people go up for prayer at the end of a church service and have their bodies start trembling or their hands start shaking. From what I've seen over the years in deliverance, I believe these are demons manifesting. The manifestations in Toronto were not subtle, and it didn't take a rocket scientist to figure out that this kind of manifestation could not possibly be the Holy Spirit. Unfortunately, there is little teaching in the church world about the demonic and the ministry of deliverance. So understandably, many people might easily mistake demonic manifestations for Holy Spirit manifestations.

Obedience Required

Deliverance is about setting people free from the barriers that would keep them from following Christ fully and obediently.

It is not just a quick fix to relieve pain, although that can certainly be a wonderful benefit. Admittedly there are some who want that quick fix, and they have no intention of following Christ in obedience, although that is the exception rather than the rule.

When we walk in sin, it's a reproach to Christ—a slap in the face to the one who came to set us free from sin's dominion. We serve a holy God who demands obedience. Didn't Jesus say, "If anyone loves me, he'll obey my teaching" (John 14:23, NIV)?

What was Christ saying to us in that scripture? Basically, He was telling us that we should show our love for Him by walking in obedience to His commands. Isn't that the least we can do for the one who laid down His life for us? His commands are for our own good. They lead to abundant life. But the book of Romans tells us, "The wages of sin is death" (Romans 6:23, KJV). I think it's a pretty easy choice: life or death!

What kind of an example are we to the world if we're no different than the world, if we walk in the ways of the world? Some Christians just want the benefits of the kingdom minus the King—Jesus Christ, the Kings of kings and Lord of lords!

From my experience in running a deliverance ministry, I have personally seen that this is the power arm of the New Testament. I have been walking a close walk with the Lord Jesus Christ for twenty-seven years, yet I did not see any miracles until I started operating in deliverance. Since then I have seen brothers and sisters in Christ healed of every disease known to mankind. Through His wonderful ministry of deliverance, I have seen God's people set free from every captivity that Satan has put upon them. The list includes addiction to drugs, alcohol, tobacco, pornography, lust, sexual perversion, depression, eating disorders, panic attacks and multiple personality disorders.

Miraculous Healings

One young lady, who is a schoolteacher by the name of Melissa, was delivered and completely healed of the dyslexia that she'd had all of her life as she went through an individual deliverance. Another lovely elderly lady by the name of Margaret had her eyesight restored after going through the Freemasonry group deliverance.

I have a spiritual daughter, who for the sake of anonymity I'll call Sarah, who was raised in a spirit-filled church and went through every healing line and received prayer by many great evangelists that came through the churches. Yet she never received a healing for panic attacks, depression, and scoliosis until she came to Isaiah 61 and received deliverance. She is now set free.

Her problems stemmed from childhood—she was raised with a lot of trauma and fear in an alcoholic household. After inner healing and the casting out of the demons that came in through those open doors, she was set free. Her husband is a youth pastor, and they travel a lot in his ministry. The panic attacks were so bad that if they were on a road trip, halfway there she'd get a panic attack, and they'd have to turn around and come back home. Now she can travel all over the state of Arizona and even to Mexico without any problems because "Whom the son sets free is free indeed!" (John 8:36). Her case is one of thousands.

RECOGNIZING SATAN'S SCHEMES

"Be sober, be vigilant; because your adversary the devil, as a roaring lion, walketh about, seeking whom he may devour" (1 Peter 5:8, KJV)

While a large segment of the church denies the reality of demons, those that acknowledge the demonic will usually justify their belief by rationalizing that they must be everywhere except in America. I always say, "Here in America, the demons just wear business suits." When I was a young Christian, I heard from those in my church that to talk about spiritual warfare or the demonic doesn't glorify Jesus but rather glorifies Satan. I was to just "praise Jesus," and everything would be fine.

Well, I did that, and as I was just praising Jesus, the devil got one of my loved ones. All because I had not been taught that we're in a battle with the enemy of our souls. Also the fact that the battle will be there until the day we go home to be with the Lord or the rapture takes place, whichever comes first. Satan and his hordes of hell never take a holiday. Their whole desire is to populate hell and if they can't do that, they bring the maximum amount of harassment into our lives. I also didn't have any knowledge of generational curses and how they operate in our lives, despite the fact that I'd attended many different Christian churches. No one taught on this much-needed truth. I didn't know that despite how well you raise your children, generational curses and patterns, if left unbroken, are very powerful and will be repeated as they reach adulthood.

Satan's Snare for Marriages

I can tell you from what I have personally witnessed in a family member's life that one of the greatest traps Satan sets for young people is bringing the wrong person into their lives. This is especially true if the young person has a calling on his life. Satan will then set a snare for him or her by using unbroken generational curses of lust, bad companions, and bad marriages to thwart his or her calling. Satan knows full well that if he can get him ensnared into an ungodly relationship or marriage, he can get him or her completely off of God's pathway and onto a pathway of sin with the ultimate goal being a complete circumvention of that young person's calling and destiny.

That is why it is so critical that you pray every day for God's choice of a mate for you or your children. I am already praying and proclaiming that my grandchildren will all marry their God-appointed mates so that they can fulfill their destinies in God. In addition to prayer, look at your family history and see what's been in operation and break those generational curses over your children and grandchildren. I will outline that more fully in the final chapter of this book.

We need to be cognizant of the fact that there are two invisible kingdoms ever locked in mortal combat over the soul and destiny of mankind—the kingdom of darkness and the kingdom of light, Satan's kingdom and God's kingdom. Everything that happens to us in the natural realm is first determined in the invisible or spiritual realm.

Schemes to Destroy God's Anointed

It seems that the demonic realm recognizes the anointing of God on someone's life from the time of birth, and they will set out to destroy that person in order to keep him or her from his or her calling. We're all born with a destiny and a purpose, but some are born with a calling, and that is to be mightily used in God's kingdom. Those are the ones Satan and his cohorts will set out to destroy. Remember in Exodus chapter one when Pharaoh gave the order that every boy born to the Israelites was to be killed? Who do you think was behind that order? The devil wanted to destroy Moses who was born to be a deliverer to his people. However, we see that God foiled his plan because God is omnipotent, omniscient, and omnipresent; Satan is not. God knows all things, and He sees all things. Satan's knowledge is limited as well as his power, and he certainly is not omnipresent. He can only be in one place at a time, unlike God. God will always checkmate Satan! He will also use the things that Satan means for harm in our lives and turn it to good.

We see the same exact plot being implemented by Satan in the New Testament. When King Herod heard that a baby was born who was to be King of the Jews, he ordered that every boy born in Bethlehem and its vicinity who was two years old or younger be killed. An angel of the Lord appeared to Joseph in a dream and warned him to get up, take the child and Mary, and escape to Egypt until they received further instructions. Once again, God checkmated Satan. Satan never comes up with anything new. He just uses the same strategies over and over again because he's not a creator; he's just an imitator. He's a counterfeiter and a usurper.

Satan is particularly interested in destroying males, especially firstborn males, since they carry the family name. He loves to pervert the bloodline while God wants to restore the bloodline. There's also the fact that God has established laws wherein the first fruit of everything is to be dedicated to Him; that includes the fruit of the womb. As a result, Satan always tries to steal the firstborn. If he can't destroy the firstborn, his second best strategy is to get them to reject God and thus serve him.

God's Intervention

I can tell you from my own life that I was born with an anointing, and the devil tried at least four times to destroy me. The first time was when I was nine months old, and we were living in Europe. My mother was American but had married a European man. When Hitler began to take over much of Europe, my father became an underground freedom fighter. He was ultimately caught by the Nazis and executed. Then the Nazis came after my mother, my sister, and myself; they would have killed us as well, but because my mother was an American citizen, their plot was foiled, and my mother brought us back to the U.S. Then there was an automobile accident right after I was saved where we would have been in a head-on collision had God not intervened. An angel of the Lord picked up my car and set it down again, miraculously sparing my life, the life of my son, and one daughter.

At the very first Christian church I attended after my salvation experience, a demonized woman whom I didn't even know attacked me in the foyer of the church after the service. I had wept throughout the service as I heard, for the first time in my life, teaching from God's Word, the Bible. I was so excited and happy to have found what I'd been looking for all of my life. Then the unspeakable happened. As I was talking to others in the foyer and feeling so blessed to be there, a woman came flying at me through the crowd and tried to physically assault me. The demons saw the anointing on me before I even had a clue as to what was happening.

Satan and his hordes of hell also study our temperament and are familiar with our weaknesses and vulnerabilities. They use these to ensnare us with the ultimate goal being to prevent us from serving Christ. The greater the calling, the greater the number of demons assigned to us with the objective of thwarting that calling.

The Need for Vigilance

While it is imperative that we walk in love, we must at the same time not neglect the fact that we are in a battle. Paul the apostle tells us over and over again that we are in a battle with the enemy of our souls and instructs us to put on the full armor of God. Why would we need armor if we weren't in a battle? What natural army in the world goes to war against their enemies without first carefully studying the enemy, understanding their habits, their terrain, their strengths and weaknesses, and then devising a methodical battle plan against them? We, as God's army, also need to study the enemy so as to not become a victim. We can only be victorious in this spiritual war we are in by knowing the enemy's ways. We are to stand our ground, advance the kingdom, and walk all over the enemy—upsetting his plans, purposes, and strategies. Didn't Jesus say in Luke 10:19, "Behold I give you power to tread on serpents and scorpions, and over all the power of the enemy and nothing shall by any means harm you"?

We must be ever mindful of the fact that the enemy's position is vulnerable. That is only an established fact for those who are willing to engage in aggressive warfare. Once we arise in our authority, we will then see that we are able to dictate the terms of the battle, not Satan and his hordes. Just as a natural army never wins battles or a war by simply being on the defense, so it is with a spiritual army. We cannot afford to be passive, thus giving the victory to the enemy by default. God's people must stop being doormats for Satan. Christ's triumph over Satan is full and complete, and he has deputized his body of believers—giving us his power of attorney to enforce that victory and triumph!

The Holy Spirit gave me a dream enforcing the reality of the need for God's people to always be on the offense against the enemy and to arise and be the soldiers in the army of the Lord that the Apostle Paul depicted for us in Ephesians six.

In the dream, I saw an oceanfront with a lovely beach. On the beach were hundreds and hundreds of people, sunning and just enjoying themselves. As I watched, all of a sudden I saw a group of fierce warriors on horses with swords drawn, coming down a slope, headed for the beach. They looked like the fierce warriors in the movie *Braveheart*.

Then, to my horror, I saw them attacking the vacationers on the beach, completely massacring them. It was a frightening scene. The Holy Spirit was confirming the reality of what I've been teaching in my services—that the enemy never takes a holiday like God's people do. The fact is that he's attacking most of us and bringing complete destruction into our lives while we are totally unaware of who's behind our problems. We must be like David—worshippers and warriors—always vigilant against the enemy. There is a time for worship and a time for battle, and we must never get out of balance by focusing on one to the exclusion of the other.

When I was a young Christian, I was taught, "Therefore if anyone is in Christ, he is a new creation; old things have passed away; behold all things have become new" (2 Corinthians 5:17, NKJV). I was told that we are to "Forget those things that are behind" (Philippians 3:13, NKJV). The scriptures are absolutely correct, however, the application is not, because the reality is that you cannot forget those things until they are properly dealt with. And stuffing unresolved issues from your childhood will only cause depression, anger, and sickness in adulthood. Wounded children result in grownup pain.

If those childhood issues are not resolved, we will spend all of our adult life reacting in dysfunctional, self-destructive ways. I deal with multitudes of people who are born again and serving the Lord yet are struggling with unresolved issues from their childhood. Or they are struggling with the consequences of ancestral/generational curses operating in their lives. All of which are severely impeding their destinies and callings, not to mention their walk with the Lord.

What does the following scripture actually mean? "If any man is in Christ, he is a new creation; the old has passed away and all things have become new" (2 Corinthians 5:17).

Does this scripture mean that once a person is a Christian, he's not going to struggle any more with the issues he had before? That is absolutely not true, and the thousands of Christians I've ministered deliverance to can attest to that. What that scripture is telling us is that the moment we become a Christian, our spirit has been born again of God, and our alienation from God has completely passed away.

However, we now have to start cleaning up the consequences of damage that has been done in the past, both through our own personal sin before Christ and through the sins of our ancestors. It is only through the ministry of healing and deliverance—following salvation—that the work of the enemy and the result of having inherited our ancestors' sins can now be undone. This process of restoration can only begin when a person becomes a new creation in Christ Jesus.

Many of the things we go through require spiritual warfare. The word of God tells us, "The heavens, even the highest heavens, belong to God, but the earth He has given to mankind" (Psalm 115:16).

So what happens on this earth is up to us. The victory has been won for us at Calvary. God could have put Satan completely away, but he chose to allow him to carry on in order to give the body of Christ training in overcoming—training for reigning—to have the Church of Jesus Christ enforce the victory of Calvary. How do we learn to be overcomers if we have nothing to overcome? How do we learn to be warriors for the Lord, if we don't have battles to engage in? If we don't enforce God's will, Satan has his way. We see that everywhere in our culture. Satan has taken over much of the media, our schools, and our government. Why? Because God's people didn't arise and say, "No you don't, Satan! You cannot have our schools, you cannot have our media, and you cannot have our government! We take them back for our God and for His Christ!" In fact, oftentimes, the ground that Christians possessed in previous generations has been yielded to the enemy due to spiritual apathy among believers. The enemy will always be right there to advance his purposes if the Christians are not vigilant in holding their ground and advancing kingdom purposes. "The kingdoms of the world have become the kingdom of our Lord and of His Christ" (Revelation 11:15). It's up to us to enforce God's word and his will on the earth.

GOD'S WILL?

Sadly, most Christian's think it is God's will when bad things happen in our lives. Too often I've heard comments such as, "Oh well, if God wants me to lose my house and start over again, that's fine." Or, "I guess God is trying to teach me something through this infirmity." Or, "I guess God needed my sister/wife/husband in heaven." While God can cause all things to work together for the good in our lives according to Romans 8:28, many times the hardships we suffer are signs of curses in operation. These could be curses of poverty, curses of homelessness, curses of infirmity, or curses of premature death just to name a few. Nonetheless, God always brings good out of bad. He is the greatest recycler in the universe.

"What does it profit a man to gain the whole world and lose his soul?" (Mark 8:36). There may be times when God is trying to break a person's pride, arrogance, independence, and rebellion against Him. It is possible that He may allow a person to lose his home, wealth, and possessions if the person has made an idol out of those things. God will never cause a loved one to be taken prematurely. That is a curse of premature death in operation. He is a loving God; He knows that if we place too much importance on these other things I mentioned, they will lead us away from Him and down a path of destruction. God loves us so much He is willing to do anything to get and hold our attention. David said, "It was good for me to be afflicted that I might learn your decrees" (Psalm 119:71).

However, if you are walking in obedience to God's Word and ways and that type of thing happens, there may be a curse in operation. The other scenario is that as you advance in God's kingdom, He will use the afflictions of life as a part of our sanctification process in preparation to be used for a great purpose in His kingdom, in order that we will be a worthy vessel for the Master's use. So we see that there are three possibilities for these types of things to be happening in our lives:

1. God is dealing with us because we're in rebellion against Him in these areas.

2. God has you in a refiner's fire so that He can remove all the "dross" (things that are ungodly) out of you and make you fit for the calling that is on your life.

3. There are unbroken ancestral/generational curses in operation in our lives. If that's the case, then spiritual warfare is required.

If you spend time in prayer and seeking God, He will reveal which one of these three things is in operation in your life. Anything that cycles over and over again is a curse in operation, i.e. joblessness, homelessness, infirmity, and divorce. You can rest assured that you will be put in a refiner's fire if God has shown you that there is a calling on your life or if you've asked God to be used for healing, deliverance, miracles, evangelism, etc.

If you are a professing Christian but walking in blatant sin against God's Word and ways or if *things* have become more important than God, rest assured that He will remove those *things*. If we know that it's God's dealing, we submit to it. If we're in sin, we repent. If it's the enemy, we do spiritual battle.

I don't believe that infirmity and disease are ever from God, or else Jesus Christ would have been the biggest rebel that ever lived. The Bible says, "He went about healing *all* who were *oppressed* by the devil" (Acts 10:38, NKJV). Sickness and infirmity are a curse, and it may be generational (something coming down the bloodline) or due to sin in your life where you've opened a door for the devil to attack you. That scripture is pretty clear; sickness and disease are of the devil! Accidents that cause crippling or maiming are always the result of unbroken ancestral/generational curses in operation. Many times they are Freemasonry curses, which I'll explain in another chapter.

GENERATIONAL AND ANCESTRAL CURSES

As I dove into the deliverance ministry, I discovered from interviews with clients that generational patterns were being re-enacted over and over again in their families. It quickly became apparent that ninety-nine percent of the issues we were dealing with were generational in nature. It also became quite apparent that unless these were renounced and broken, the patterns would just continue on in the bloodline, bringing curses in the lives of their descendants. With each generation, they seemed to gain strength.

One of the major ways that curses are transmitted is through our bloodline. Our ancestral lineage determines the particular "flavor" of our sins and desires. I often liken generational sin to a duck. Just as a duck is drawn to water, so we will be drawn to the sins of our ancestors. There will be that strong iniquitous pull toward that particular sin(s).

In some families the ancestral lineage is addiction, and that can cover anything from addiction to alcohol, nicotine, sex, and pornography. In other families it may be sexual perversion. In yet another family the spirits that have followed that family may be eating disorders or strife and contention. Other families may have a huge spirit of infirmity that has come down the bloodline, causing repeated sickness and disease in the descendants. Yet another family may have poverty and chronic financial problems or failures that have been over their generations or unexplainable accidents and premature death. Another family may have mental illness that has affected generations.

Whatever types of spirits have been in your family and continue to flourish in the succeeding generations, there is a root cause for that particular failure in your family. Someone in the bloodline opened the door for those spirits to enter in through some sort of sin. Sin is the gateway or the open door for the curse. The sin gave the spirits a legal right to that ancestor and subsequently to his bloodline and will continue on unhindered until found out. Once found out and repented of, they lose their legal right to that bloodline, and the demons behind those curses can now be cast out.

Ancestral/generational curses are carried by familiar spirits that know our family history better than we do. They may have been in our bloodline for hundreds or thousands of years. I've had many generational or ancestral demons scream at me, "I'm not leaving. I have a right to this bloodline. I've been in this bloodline for hundreds, or they'll say thousands of years, and you can't make me go." Of course, after I have each person repent of the ancestral sin—whether lust, rage, or witchcraft—the demon has to go because its legal right has been taken away. They will fight to stay in that bloodline by refusing to let the client speak, controlling their tongue so that they can't speak. They don't want to leave the "home" they've had for so long.

These familiar spirits' assignment is to transmit to us the propensities, desires, or strong tendencies from past generations. They may cause you to behave in certain ways or have particular mannerisms. These generational spirits are transferred to us right in the womb so that from birth onward we will have that pull toward the sins of our ancestors until we act out what they practiced.

We will think it's just a part of our personality until the moment that we become aware of the working of generational or ancestral spirits. That is an unprecedented moment of revelation for Christians. It certainly was for me. All of a sudden everything seemed to make sense to me for the first time in my life. I can tell you I have heard that sentiment expressed thousands of times as people have heard my teachings on generational/ancestral curses, and even more so after they've gone through deliverance from these curses and found the freedom they'd been seeking all of their lives!

Expounding on the subject of familiar spirits, I will share with you some personal history. As I stated earlier, the Nazis killed my dad when I was nine months old. Therefore, I never really knew my dad. I never had the opportunity to observe his mannerisms or imitate them. Here is the interesting observation, which will validate what I said about familiar spirits transmitting to the next generation certain behaviors and mannerisms. I remember as a child my mother telling me that I acted just like my father. She said I even had certain mannerisms when eating that was just like my dad. That's very interesting; wouldn't you say, in light of the fact that I never knew my dad?

Just as godliness multiplies with each generation, so it is with wickedness. I now teach what I have personally gleaned from the Word of God and many years of experience in ministry: we are all the product of our ancestors, both physically and spiritually. We carry their physical genetics as well as their spiritual genetics.

By going backward on the generational chart, each of us has two parents, four grandparents, eight great-grandparents and sixteen great-great grandparents—a total of thirty ancestors from which curses have possibly derived. By looking at the cause for curses in this light, it is easy to see how we could be suffering all sorts of curses due to ancestral sins.

To give you a vivid illustration of wickedness increasing with each generation as well as godliness, there was a published study of two well-known American families of the 19th century:

The first is Max Jukes, who was an atheist, and who married a godless woman. Some 560 descendants were traced. Of these 310 died as paupers; 150 became criminals, 7 of them murderers; 100 were known to be drunkards. More than half the women were prostitutes. In all, the descendants cost the United States Government 1.25 million 19th century dollars.

The second is Jonathan Edwards who was a contemporary of Max Jukes. He was a committed Christian who married a godly young lady. Some 1,394 descendants were traced, of these:

295 graduated from college, from whom 13 became college presidents, and 65 became professors; 3 were elected as U.S. Senators, 3 as State Governors, and others sent as ministers to foreign countries; 30 were judges, 100 were lawyers, one the dean of an outstanding law school; 56 became physicians, one was dean of a medical school; 75 became officers in the Army and Navy; 100 were well known missionaries, preachers, and prominent authors; another 80 held some form of public office, of whom 3 were mayors of large cities. One was Comptroller of the US Treasury, another a Vice-President of the United States. Not one of the descendants of the Edwards family was a liability to the government.

This is pretty clear evidence of blessing and honor going to those who serve God and are committed Christians. Also evidence of what not serving God brings into the human life as evidenced by the descendants of Max Jukes and his godless wife. Deuteronomy 30:19: "...I have set before you life and death, blessing and cursing; therefore choose life, that both you and your descendants may live."

Let's bring that into our present lives. What is the first thing that a doctor does when you go into his office with a malady? He asks you your physical family history, doesn't he? He inquires as to what types of things were in your generational line, i.e. diabetes or cancer. We, at Isaiah 61 Ministries, do the same thing. Except we ask you your spiritual history—what types of sins were your ancestors involved in? Was there alcoholism, abuse, or involvement in the occult (tarot card readings, going to psychics, séances, superstitions, Ouija board, table tipping,)? Are there destructive personality traits and behavior patterns, abuse (physical, emotional, or sexual), suicidal tendencies, anger, poverty, mental illness, female problems, i.e. menstrual problems, inability to conceive, marital problems, or divorce?

In taking the history of those who come in for ministry, I have discovered that the patterns or flavor of sin in the parents, grandparents, and great grandparents were almost always carried out by the subsequent generations. One lady who came in for ministry put it this way, "I have felt all my life like I was living under a dark cloud that I could not come out from under no matter what I did." That was a pretty good description of what it is to live under the weight of unbroken generational curses. Anything that cycles over and over again in your life and you just cannot seem to get rid of is a curse in operation. A person under a curse cannot escape through human ingenuity because a curse is a spiritual problem that cannot be remedied by natural means.

In the book of Jeremiah it says, "You show loving kindness to thousands, and repay the iniquity of the fathers into the bosom of their children after them" (Jeremiah 32:18, NKJV).

In the book of Exodus it says, in speaking of worshipping idols or other gods, "For I, the Lord thy God, am a jealous

God, visiting the iniquity of the fathers on the children to the third and fourth generations of those who hate me, but showing mercy to thousands, to those who love Me and keep My commandments" (Exodus 20:5, NKJV). In another portion of Exodus, it says this: " ... visiting the iniquity of the fathers upon the children and the children's children to the third and fourth generation" (Exodus 34:7, NKJV).

All of these scriptures tell us that the iniquity of the fathers is passed on to the children.

These scriptures also show us the gravity of sins of the fathers, also, of course, the mothers. Sin affects not only those who commit it but also the generations to come. This shows us the terrible consequences of sin. Sin is more than an isolated act. It can reverberate for generations to come.

Because the Jews witnessed the operation of generational curses throughout Bible history, they devised a proverb to describe the effects of a father's sin being passed down. We see in Ezekiel 18:2 where they said "The fathers have eaten sour grapes, and the children's teeth are set on edge." Then we go over to Jeremiah 31:29, where the Prophet Jeremiah declares the Word of the Lord "In those days people will no longer say, 'The fathers have eaten sour grapes, and the children's teeth are set on edge." This is a prophetic scripture pointing to the time of Christ, when people could be set free from the father's sins by the name and blood of Jesus *if* they chose to appropriate this benefit of the cross. When you look at the context of that scripture, you see that God is talking about the days when He will make a new covenant with the house of Israel and the house of Judah; he would put his law in their minds and write it on their hearts. That's the New Covenant or the New Testament, i.e. the time of Christ.

Sometimes one particular generational curse will skip one generation but land in the next. Let me give you an example of that:

My daughter Lisa's friend was sharing with her a concern she had with her daughter Stephanie. She told my daughter that from the time Stephanie turned thirteen she started having this irrational fear of being raped. So I told my daughter it was probably a generational curse in operation and told her to have her friend call me. When she did, as she started to tell me about this fear that had come upon Stephanie, seemingly out of nowhere, I immediately stopped her. I told her that I guaranteed that someone in either her or her husband's bloodline had been raped at exactly the same age and that this generational spirit was operating in her daughter. She gasped as she said, "Oh my gosh. I just remembered as you were speaking that my grandmother told me, years ago, that she had been raped at age thirteen." She then asked me if it could skip a generation, as she herself had never had that same thing. I assured her it could. So we set up an appointment, and I broke the curse and called the spirit out of her; the problem was resolved.

I want to give you one of the best-documented true stories that vividly illustrates how generational or ancestral curses work. This was a news article that appeared in the *Dallas Morning News* on October 20, 1997, entitled "Crimes of the Father."

It told parallel stories about Darrel Hill, a fifty-seven-year-old convicted killer who sat on death row in an Arkansas prison, and his son, Jeffrey Landrigan, a thirty-seven-year-old convicted killer who sat on death row in an Arizona prison. The Hill family had a long history of bootlegging, alcoholism, and violent crime.

According to the article, Darrel Hill last saw his son thirty-five years ago when he was a young junkie, locked up on a burglary charge. His son, Billy, was a baby on a jailhouse visit, nestled in his mother's arms. Soon afterwards, Billy was adopted into a very stable, affluent family. He was given a new name, Jeffrey Landrigan, and what seemed to be a chance for a better life.

Hill, a third-generation criminal, continued his family's legacy of lawlessness. In 1980, after several stints in prison, he murdered a state game warden during a gas station robbery and wound up on Arkansas' death row.

Although he grew up as Jeff Landrigan, Billy remained his father's son. A self-described misfit in the middle-class life he was given, he turned to a life of alcohol and drugs. One thousand and one hundred miles and three decades removed, he sat on Arizona's death row, a two-time killer, just like the father he never knew.

Jeff never knew his father, yet he followed in his father's and his ancestors' footsteps. A prisoner in jail with Jeff in Arizona had previously been in jail in Arkansas and recognized the similarities between the two men. This is how Landrigan learned the identity of his birth father.

Jeff's birth mother was quoted as saying, "They look alike, talk alike, sound alike, and think alike. It's mind-blowing." Yet these two men have never met face to face and never knew each other.

Knowledge about generational curses could have spared Jeff going down the same path as the dad he never knew. If those generational curses had been broken over young Jeff, I guarantee that he would not have fulfilled them but rather fulfilled the plans that God had for his life.

That's why it's so important for anyone adopting a baby to find out as much as they can about the birth parents and get those generational curses broken off of that baby, so it will not live out the birth parents' sins.

Many in the body of Christ believe that curses are just Old Testament rules and regulations. The truth is that they are the cause and effect principles that God has set into the universe, which will stand as long as the universe stands because God's Word and His laws are unchanging. There is much misunderstanding regarding the law. Nowhere in the Bible does it say that Jesus came to cancel the law but rather to fulfill it and to set us free from bondage.

In the Book of Matthew it tells us that Jesus came to fulfill the law:

> Do not think that I have come to abolish the Law or the Prophets; I have not come to abolish them but to fulfill them. I tell you the truth, until heaven and earth disappear, not the smallest letter, not the least stroke of a pen, will by any means disappear from the Law until everything is accomplished. Anyone who breaks one of the least of these commandments and teaches others to do the same will be called least in the kingdom of heaven, but whoever practices and teaches these commands will be called great in the kingdom of heaven.
>
> Matthew 5:17–19 (NIV)

What that scripture is showing us is that the law is still in effect today for lawbreakers, whether they're saved or unsaved. What Jesus brought to mankind is the ability to gain release from the sure penalties of the law through His finished work at the cross of Calvary. The Scriptures tell us that Christ did not come to free us from the law but rather to redeem us from the *curse* of the law that we might enjoy the blessings of Abraham, according to Galatians 3:13.

Where the confusion comes in concerning the law is this: Galatians 3:10–13 speaks of people trying to gain salvation by observing the law, as the Pharisees did. Our salvation is through faith, not by observing the law. However, that does not give us license to break God's laws; if we do, we will pay the consequences. Yes, we are living in days of grace, however that does not get us off the hook in regards to consequences. The principle of the sins of the fathers being visited on the children still stands. Pick up any newspaper today; you'll read stories where the sins of the parents are being visited upon the children.

The difference under the New Covenant is that Christ has given us the ability to deal with these things now. These curses can now be broken after repentance in the name of Jesus and by the blood of Jesus, unlike in Old Testament times. The provision is there, but it does not come automatically with the new birth. It must be appropriated. Healing is provided for us by the shed blood of Jesus, but it doesn't come automatically when we become believers. It too must be appropriated through faith, prayer, and standing on God's Word. There is a difference between the provision made for us at the cross of Calvary and the appropriation of those provisions.

Old Testament Patterns of Generational Sin

In the Old Testament, their sins could be forgiven, but the curse attached to that sin could never be broken. It had to work its way out to the third and fourth generations as outlined in Exodus, "For I, the Lord thy God, am a jealous God, visiting the iniquity of the fathers on the children to the third and fourth generations of those who hate me" (Exodus 20:5, NKJV).

In another portion of Exodus, it says, "…visiting the iniquity of the fathers upon the children and the children's children to the third and fourth generation" (Ex. 34:7, NKJV). In the book of Jeremiah it says, "You show loving kindness to thousands and repay the iniquity of the fathers into the bosom of their children after them" (Jeremiah 32:18, NKJV).

Throughout the Old Testament, you can see the pattern of generational or hereditary sin, beginning with Adam in the Garden of Eden. Through Adam's disobedience and rebellion against God's commands to him, curse entered into humanity. We see the generations following suffering as a result of Adam's sin. We see that Adam's son Cain became the first murderer recorded in the Bible, and his descendant Lamech then followed suit.

We can look at the life of Abraham, who is called the father of the faith, and we can see some generational curses that he set in motion for his descendants. First and foremost is when God promised him a son and an heir; he grew impatient after many years of waiting for the fulfillment of the promise. He then did what many Christians are still doing today. He thought he'd help God out. So with Sarah's consent, he took her handmaid, Hagar, as his wife, who then gave him a son named Ishmael. Ishmael was a child of the flesh and represents a counterfeit. He became the father of the modern Arab nations. The name Ishmael means "man of war."

Later, when the promise was fulfilled and Sarah gave birth to the promised child and heir, Isaac, there was conflict between the son of promise and the child of the flesh. That conflict is still going on in this day and age between the Jews and the Arabs, who are ever in conflict over the inheritance.

We also see the beginning of some interesting generational curses unfold as a direct consequence of Abraham's actions. We see that Isaac, who was the younger, was given the birthright over Ishmael, who was the elder. This generational curse of the elder son losing his birthright to the younger son followed Abraham's descendants for four succeeding generations. After Ishmael lost his birthright to Isaac, Esau forfeited his, then Reuben, and finally Manassah. In the Old Testament, the birthright was a very important matter and was to be given to the eldest son.

Abraham also initiated another generational curse when he deceived Pharaoh concerning his wife, Sarah, in Genesis 12:18–19. Because Sarah was so beautiful, Abraham was afraid that if Pharaoh knew she was his wife, he'd have Abraham killed in order to take Sarah into his harem. So what did he do? He told Sarah to lie for him and say he was her brother. As you remember, Pharaoh then took Sarah into his harem, but before he had a chance to touch her, God warned him very strongly in a dream that he was taking Abraham's wife. He told him if he slept with her he was as good as dead! Pharaoh pleaded with God, stating his innocence and ignorance of the truth about Sarah, and then he returned Sarah to Abraham the next day, without laying a hand on her. Pharaoh was very angry with Abraham.

Well, guess what? Isaac fulfilled that generational curse of deception with the same king under the exact same set of circumstances with his wife, Rebekah. We then see that same curse of deception operating in Jacob and Jacob's sons. Remember when Jacob's sons deceived Jacob regarding what happened to his favorite son, Joseph? As I said, in the Old Testament, the curses would just have to work their way out to the third and fourth generations, but they could not be broken until the New Covenant in which Jesus shed His blood and gave us the ability to break the curses of our forefathers.

"The Lord is longsuffering, and of great mercy, forgiving iniquity and transgression, and by no means clearing the guilty, visiting the iniquity of the fathers upon the children unto the third and fourth generation" (Numbers 14:18, NKJV).

What that scripture shows us is what I just stated above. There was forgiveness of sin available in the Old Testament, but the curse attached to the sin could not be broken until the time of Christ. It would just have to work its way out to the third and fourth generation as these Bible stories show us.

When we look at the life of David, we see *his* sins being visited upon his children. Remember in 2 Samuel 12:9–13 when David committed adultery with Bathsheba and had her husband Uriah the Hittite killed? God loved David, and the Bible even says that David was a man after God's own heart. But when he committed those sins, God sent the Prophet Nathan to David to warn him of the gravity of his sins and the curse that he had brought upon his house/bloodline. He told David that because of what he had done, the sword would never depart from his house.

We know that David immediately repented, and God forgave him his sins. But we also see the curse of destruction and lust following his children. A perfect example of one's sins being forgiven, but the curse continuing in the bloodline. While one son Amnon raped his own sister through a great deal of treachery, his other son, Absalom, rose up in rebellion against David. We also see that spirit of lust that drove David to sin with Bathsheba passed onto David's son Solomon and magnified. Solomon had seven hundred wives and three hundred concubines.

There is an excellent scripture in the New Testament showing the reality of generational curses:

> Now as Jesus passed by, He saw a man who was blind from birth, and His disciples asked Him saying, 'Rabbi, who sinned, this man or his parents, that he was born blind?' Jesus answered, 'Neither this man nor his parents sinned, but that the works of God should be revealed in him.'
>
> John 9:1–3 (NKJV)

Jesus was not denying the reality of generational curses; He was basically saying that in this case this was not the cause.

God wanted to work a miracle in this man's life. I don't believe that there is anything in the Bible without a reason. I believe that this portion of Scripture is in the Word to show us that the disciples in Jesus's day understood the concept of generational curses, and Jesus was affirming that concept.

All of these case studies of the operation of generational curses in the Old Testament show us that there are indeed spiritual laws governing curses and that curses don't just float around in the atmosphere like a leaf blown by the wind and then just land on someone. Someone does not just come under a curse by happenstance. There are basic spiritual laws that govern curses, just as there are basic spiritual laws that govern the universe. There must be a cause, a legal right.

In the book of Proverbs it says, "Like a flitting sparrow, like a flying swallow, so a curse without cause shall not alight" (Proverbs 26:2). This scripture gives an excellent correlation of divine principles that govern the whole of the universe, both the visible world and the invisible—the unseen spiritual realm.

We know scientists have studied the migration of swallows and ducks and geese, to name a few, trying to discover how they can leave one part of the country or one continent, travel to another, spend the winter, and then miraculously find their way back to their original nests and locations. We also know they don't have the answers, but for anyone who knows God, there is an answer. The answer is that these birds are guided by something that was put inside them by the Creator of the universe. In the same way, curses are guided by laws the Creator of the universe has put into place.

The question then arises: does ignorance of God's laws exempt me from the consequences of breaking those laws? In other words, if I don't know what God's laws and his commands are and I break those laws, am I still going to suffer consequences? The answer to that is yes. Ignorance of God's laws and commands does not exempt us from the penalties of breaking those laws anymore than ignorance of the laws of our land exempts us from the penalties of breaking those laws. For those who belong to Christ, we can immediately ask forgiveness and put that transgression under the Blood.

Demons are Satan's foot soldiers, and they are enforcers of curses. They constantly tempt us to sin against God so they can gain entrance into us and create strongholds of sin in our lives in the hopes that those sins will eventually lead us away from Christ and lead us to hell. Demons cannot just arbitrarily enter into us. They have to have a legal right, an open door, as I established in the previous chapter. Sin is an open door. That's why every person has many demons assigned to them to tempt and seduce on a continual basis. They never give up and are relentless in their pursuit of the souls of men.

Demons know they must abide by the laws that God has put into the universe, and they dare not cross those laws. When we step outside of the parameters of our covenant with God, we step right into Satan's kingdom, and he delights in that. When we disobey God's commands in His Word, we open ourselves up to demonic invasion in our lives. Even those that are not in God's kingdom are subject to God's laws. The law is in effect for lawbreakers, both saved and unsaved.

As stated earlier, ignorance of God's laws does not protect us from the consequences of breaking those laws. A good analogy of that is this: suppose you were driving down a street going fifty-five miles per hour and all of a sudden a police officer pulls you over. He asks you, "Do you know you were going fifty-five in a zone marked twenty-five miles per hour?" Your answer is, "But, officer, I didn't see the sign!" Do you think it's going to keep you from getting that speeding ticket? I don't think so. It is the same with God's laws. The laws of sowing and reaping are in effect in the whole of creation, applying to both the natural world and spiritual world. Galatians 6:7–8 says, "Be not deceived; God is not mocked; for whatsoever a man soweth, that shall he also reap. For he that soweth to his flesh shall of the flesh reap corruption; but he that soweth to the Spirit shall of the Spirit reap life everlasting." (KJV).

BLESSINGS AND CURSES

If you study the Old Testament, you will see the pattern of blessing and curse. When God's people stopped following the one true God and followed the gods of the Amorites, Moabites, Syrians, and Egyptians, God would turn them over to the enemy. It was their choice—that was who they chose to follow. They knowingly sinned against God by breaking the first commandment God had given Moses on Mt. Sinai: "Thou shalt have no other gods before me" (Exodus 20:3, KJV).

The greatest sin of the Old Testament was the sin of idolatry—worshipping other gods. The consequence was always the same—enemy captivity. It is the same today when we stop following Jesus Christ; we come into enemy captivity.

After they were in captivity for a while and when they would be sick and dying, they would finally cry out to God, and He would send them a deliverer. What a loving God! When we step outside the commands of God, we open ourselves up to the devil's "blessing," and Satan is a hard, cruel taskmaster.

In the twenty-eighth chapter of Deuteronomy, we see the promises of blessings from God for obedience, and we also see the outline of curses promised for disobedience. God never does anything without first warning His people; usually, because His very nature is long-suffering and merciful, He will give many warnings to try and get us to repent before He turns us over to our enemy whom we have at that point chosen to serve.

Then because of his great love for his creation, mankind, He goes on to say in Deuteronomy, "This day I call heaven and earth as witnesses against you, that I have set before you life and death, blessings and curses. Now choose life, so that you and your children may live, and that you may love the Lord your God, and listen to His voice and hold fast to Him" (Deuteronomy 30:19, NKJV). He *pleads* with His people to choose life, to choose the pathway of blessings. That is His desire and His heart for us, but when we have rebellion against Him in our hearts, there is nothing more He can do for us. It is our choice.

Blessings and curses operate by predetermined laws in the same way that God has established the natural laws of creation, such as the law of gravity or the natural laws of sowing and reaping. Anyone, whether a believer in Christ, or unbeliever, will reap the effects in their spirit, soul, body, and life when they come into conflict with these laws. As I said before, ignorance of the law doesn't exempt us from the consequences of breaking the law.

I'm going to pull out just a few of the curses that are promised to those who disobey God's laws. As I do this, keep in mind that God pleads with His creation to choose life. He longs for His creation to be blessed. Just as there are consequences for breaking laws in our society, so there are consequences for breaking God's laws and rebelling against our Creator. Any good earthly father will set boundaries for his children as he is raising them. He knows that if he doesn't set those boundaries and if he doesn't deal with rebellion and wrong attitudes, the law will when that child grows up. Our prisons are filled with people who were raised with no boundaries or discipline.

The Bible tells us that a loving father disciplines his children and chastens them for their own good. God is a loving heavenly Father!

In the book of Deuteronomy it says:

> But it shall come to pass, if you do not obey the voice of the Lord your God, to observe carefully all His commandments and His statutes which I command you today, that all these curses will come upon you and over take you: Cursed shall you be in the city, and cursed shall you be in the country. Cursed shall be your basket and your kneading bowl. Cursed shall be the fruit of your body, i.e., our offspring/our children, and the produce of your land, the increase of your cattle and the offspring of your flocks. Cursed shall you be when you come in, and cursed shall you be when you go out. The Lord will send on you cursing, confusion, and rebuke in all that you set your hand to do, until you are destroyed and until you perish quickly, because of the wickedness of your doings in which you have forsaken me.
>
> Deuteronomy 28:15–20 (NKJV)

It then continues:

> The Lord will strike you with consumption, with fever, with inflammation, with severe burning fever, with the sword, with scorching, and with mildew; they shall pursue you until you perish.
>
> The Lord will strike you with madness and blindness and confusion of heart. And you shall grope at noonday, as a blind man gropes in darkness; you shall not prosper in your ways; you shall be only oppressed and plundered continually, and no one shall save you
>
> Deuteronomy 28:22 (NKJV)

It's pretty serious stuff, being under a curse. Let's look at some curses we see outlined in Deuteronomy 28 which mankind has brought upon himself. How has he brought these upon himself? By breaking God's laws. Insanity, poverty, failure, blindness, being stolen from, being under constant oppression, premature death, constant financial woes, to name a few.

The good news is that if we have Jesus Christ as our Lord and Savior, He has given us the ability to break any of the curses outlined. We can be set free by repenting of any known sins. Then we can break the curses attached to those sins. Then we can command the demons that are enforcing those curses to leave us in the name of Jesus Christ, the name that is above every name!

CAN A CHRISTIAN HAVE A DEMON?

One of the biggest lies the devil has floated in the Christian Church is that a Christian cannot have a demon, thus enabling him and his network of demons to continue their vile work in people's lives.

Derek Prince, a mighty general of God, who had a powerful deliverance ministry that spanned decades, said that a major denomination branded him a heretic because he was casting demons out of Christians. His response was, "What are we supposed to do? Leave the demons in them?"

Dr. Ed Murphy, in his book *The Handbook for Spiritual Warfare*, states, "a theology of Satan and demons that is both true and useful for ministry cannot be developed by theologians studying their Hebrew and Greek Bibles while sitting in their air-conditioned offices apart from some personal experience."

He goes on to say that he as well as many other theology professors, Bible teachers, counselors, missionaries and pastors in the past few years accepted what they were taught. Then they were launched into ministry and their theology put to the test of experience. They had to examine anew certain dimensions of their unreflective theology when it did not prove congruent with their own valid experience with God, with people, and, in many cases with Satan and demons.

He says, "To declare that theology must be maintained even if it is challenged by on-going experience is legalism, pharisaism, dogmatism and evidence of subtle arrogance. To continue with theology that hurts already hurting people is sin."

He says the unfortunate result worldwide is that, in general, our churches are filled with believers who are hurting through the activity of evil spirits. Many are spirit-filled believers, and yet a war rages inside of them.

If Christians cannot have demons, then why are so many Christians struggling, more often the victim than the victor? Why is there just as much addiction in the church as in the world, and why do Christians have as much sickness as non-Christians? Why are Christian marriages failing as quickly as the world? Didn't Jesus come to "give us life and that more abundantly" (John 10:10)? Where is the abundant life?

We see the fall of many ministers because deliverance is not offered to new converts. I've seen Satan bring down many powerful ministers who had a strong anointing and calling on their lives. Satan waits until that person is at the pinnacle of his success to resurrect unresolved issues from childhood so that he can bring maximum shame and disgrace to both the minister and his family and ultimately to Christianity. Ministers should not be raised up until they've gone through deliverance.

If Christians get cancer, isn't that a spirit of infirmity, and didn't Jesus cast out spirits of infirmity? If sin leads to curses—and the Bible clearly states that—and demons are enforcers of curses, then what happens to those demons that were allowed into us through the open doors of sin once we get saved? Do they just wave "bye, bye" and leave? My experience in casting thousands of demons out of Christians says otherwise. A pastor I once had used to say, "A man with an argument is at the mercy of a man with an experience." I've seen skeptics quickly change their position once they've sat in on deliverance sessions where spirit-filled believers began to manifest; then there is no more denying it.

The church's refusal to acknowledge the possibility that many of life's problems are due to demonic influence in our lives makes it easier for demons to operate undetected. Because Satan is a creature of darkness by his very nature, he does not want his activities exposed. He fights the deliverance ministry with every weapon he has. He schemes day and night to stop deliverance from coming into the church.

If the modern day church were following the pattern of Jesus, we would include the casting out of demons as a normal part of church life. The Gospel accounts show us that Jesus never sent anyone out to preach the gospel without instructing and equipping them first to cast out demons, following the pattern He established. It is abundantly clear that the New Testament pattern for evangelism ministry includes the casting out of demons. Refusing to do so is completely unscriptural. First John 3:8 says, "The Son of God appeared (came) for this purpose, that He might destroy the works of the devil" (1 John 3:8, NAS).

When you study the Bible, you will see that this is the one significant difference between the Old Testament and the New Testament—this matter of casting out of demons. In the Old Testament, we see that from Moses on, God's prophets performed many astounding miracles. Nowhere do we see where any of the prophets ever cast out a demon. It seems this was reserved for Jesus and His followers. In fact as you study the Gospel accounts, you will begin to see the correlation between healing and casting out of demons. Jesus did not separate the two—neither should the modern day church.

The heavenly Father reserved this for Jesus with the express purpose of demonstrating to mankind that there were two opposing spiritual kingdoms at work on the earth—the kingdom of God and the kingdom of Satan. It was also a clear-cut demonstration of the victory of God's kingdom over Satan's, and that was certainly not something that Satan wanted revealed. He still works furiously to keep this fact undercover. Jesus said, "But if I cast out demons by the Spirit of God, then the kingdom of God has come upon you" (Matthew.12:28, NAS).

The Benefits for Believers

Deliverance is a part of the believer's sanctification process, bringing him into healing and wholeness that God originally intended for mankind before sin entered. I believe, according to Mark 7:25–30, that deliverance and healing are "the children's bread." When the Syro-Phoenician woman pleaded with Jesus to cast a demon out of her daughter, His response was "… it is not good to take the children's bread and throw it to the little dogs" (Mark 7:27, NKJV). He was in essence saying that deliverance and casting out of demons is "the children's bread." Who are the children? It's us, the believers who belong to Jesus. Deliverance is the wonderful benefit he provided for us at the cross when He became a curse for us.

Let me ask you this. What would be the sense of casting demons out of unsaved persons or unbelievers? What would they have to keep the demons from returning? It's only believers in Jesus Christ—those that can claim Jesus Christ as their Lord and Savior—who can keep their deliverance by filling themselves up with the Word of God, the Holy Spirit, praise, and worship. These are the only things that will keep those demons from returning. Demons are darkness. In fact, they belong to the kingdom of darkness. Jesus Christ is called the light of the world, so He is light. The Word of God is divinely inspired and is light. When we're praising and worshipping God, that's light. Unsaved people don't have those things to fill themselves up after deliverance. Thus they would be seven times worse off, and it would be dangerous to do deliverance on these people.

A portion of scripture in Matthew 12 illustrates the point I'm making. It's where Jesus was talking, and he said:

> When an unclean spirit goes out of a man, he goes through dry and arid places seeking rest, and finds none. Then he says, 'I will return to my house from which I came,' and when he comes, he finds it empty, swept and put in order. Then he goes and takes with him seven other spirits more wicked than himself, and they enter and dwell there and the last state of that man is worse than the first.
>
> Matthew 12:43–45 (NKJV)

For a demon, dry and arid places are anyplace outside of a human body, as the body is comprised of fifty-five to seventy-eight per-cent water. Demons find no rest since they are unable to act out their ugly nature outside a human body. That's why they're always strategizing and plotting to get someone to sin so a door can be opened for them to have a nice home to live in. Think about it! How could a demon of alcoholism or lust or murder or abuse act out its ugly nature without a human host? It can't!

Notice that that scripture tells us that the house (or person) was swept clean (delivered of demons) and put in order, but empty (someone who is not a Christian receiving deliverance). The demon goes and brings seven more wicked spirits, and the person is worse off than before the demon was cast out. As far as I can see, that is the clearest scripture showing that deliver-ance is only for Christians.

The most often repeated argument I hear from people calling the Isaiah 61 line for help is this: "I went to my spiritual leader for help with these recurring problems, thinking that it might be demons, and he said that a Christian cannot be demon possessed." My answer is always the same: "He is absolutely correct. A Christian cannot be demon possessed as possession implies ownership."

I then go on to explain to them that when a person receives Jesus Christ as Lord and Savior, he is born again of the spirit of God and translated out of the kingdom of darkness into the kingdom of light. Ownership of their life has changed hands. From that moment on, they are rightfully possessed by the Holy Spirit of God, having been bought with a price—the precious blood of Jesus, which was shed for us at the cross of Calvary. A Christian cannot, therefore, be demon possessed. He can, however, be demonized.

Cleaning up the House

An excellent analogy comes from Peter Horrobin's book *Healing Through Deliverance.*

"If I buy a house, I possess the land it stands on—the structure of the building—*and* any defects that originated during previous ownerships; for example, termites that may be resident in the structure of the home. The same holds true if I bought a house that had rats living in the basement. I am now the new owner of a house with rats."

Those termites or rats don't automatically leave now that the house has a new owner. If I, as the new owner, don't call in a pest control company to take care of these pests, they'll just continue their destructive work in my new residence. Are you getting the picture?

Demonization in a Christian refers to those areas that the Holy Spirit has not been able to occupy because of the rats or termites that are still there. Why? Because nobody called the exterminator. This is what sanctification is—the Holy Spirit working to clean up the mess left by the previous owner who, of course, is Satan. There is no neutral ground in the world. We belong to one of two kingdoms. We belong either to the god of this world, Satan, or Jesus Christ.

Just as the termites or rats cannot be ignored, so it is with the unclean spirits that are resident in our body from our previous life—our life before we became Christians wherein we probably opened many doors for demons to enter. Some of the open doors for demons to come in are personal sin (which can include a multitude of things such as sexual sin, pornography, or alcoholism), generational sin, childhood abuse and trauma, or any brush with the occult. I will address these in greater length in another chapter of this book.

If these things are not addressed right after conversion, they will continue to operate in the new believer's life and limit the effectiveness of their Christian walk and cause a lot of problems. One of the foremost testimonies that I hear from people immediately after going through deliverance is that for the first time in their Christian walk they're able to read the Bible without falling asleep. Not only that, but the Word of God suddenly comes alive for them. I would say that not being able to read the Bible certainly limits the effectiveness of their Christian walk. I'm sure you would agree with me on that.

Most Christians would have no problem believing that unsaved people who are into all kinds of sin—such as drugs, alcoholism, sexual perversion, New Age, the occult, going to psychics, and pornography—could and probably do have demons. But what do you think happens to those demons when one of these people comes to Christ? Do they just go away? That is not biblically sound. Conversion was always accompanied by the casting out of demons. Those demons do not wave good-bye and leave. That is when the real battle begins between the two kingdoms for possession of the land or the temple, which is what the Bible calls our body.

In the book of 1 Thessalonians, it says, "Now may the God of peace Himself sanctify you completely; and may your whole spirit, soul and body be preserved blameless at the coming of our Lord Jesus Christ" (Thessalonians 5:23, NKJV). The book of Hebrews also tells us that man is a tri-part being—made up of body, soul, and spirit: "For the Word of God is living and powerful and sharper than any two-edged sword, piercing even to the division of soul and spirit and of joints and marrow…" (Thessalonians 4:12, NKJV).

When we're born again, our spirit is immediately made perfect. However, it is in the soul of man—which is comprised of mind, will, and emotions—that sanctification needs to take place. Sanctification is the process of cleaning up our temple. It is restoring, rebuilding, and refurbishing our temple. This can only happen when we get rid of the garbage that's in us, i.e. the unclean spirits from our pre-conversion days and, many times, the emotional wounding that those demons are hanging onto. Even if we gave our heart to Jesus Christ as a youngster and have followed him closely, abstaining from any overt sin, there will still be generational curses in us that need to be broken and the demons behind those cast out.

You may have walked uprightly before God all your life, but your ancestors may not have. I have addressed the issue of generational sin in a previous chapter at great length. As I mentioned in that chapter, if we go backward on the generational chart, each of us has two parents, four grandparents, eight great grandparents, and sixteen great-great grandparents. That's a total of thirty ancestors from which curses have possibly derived. How many of us know the types of sins our parents or even grandparents were into unless they were overt and obvious such as alcoholism or other obvious addictions that brought destruction to their lives.

Provision Versus Appropriation

Most of the Christian community has an understanding that because Galatians 3:13 says that we have been redeemed from the curse of the law and that Jesus Christ became a curse for us, we do not have to concern ourselves with those things that our ancestors have done, that it's automatically taken care of the moment we become a child of God, and that every curse is automatically broken. They do not understand the principle of provision versus appropriation.

Yes, Jesus Christ at the cross of Calvary became the curse for us, provided healing for every area of our lives, and most importantly provided salvation—it's all in the atonement. The provision was made! Yet those things don't automatically come to us; they have to be appropriated.

Let's look at salvation for instance. Jesus Christ made the way for the salvation of all mankind, yet is all mankind saved? No! Is it God's will for all to be saved? Yes! Just as it's God's will for all Christians to be whole, healed, and set free on every level to live the happy and abundant life that Jesus died to provide for us. The provision is there, but we have to appropriate that salvation by receiving Jesus Christ as Lord and Savior, and we must believe He is the Son of God and that He died and rose again and is seated at the right hand of the Father. So appropriation has to be made by faith.

It's the same thing with healing. Scripture tells us, "By His stripes, ye were healed" (1 Peter 2:24, KJV). It says ye *were* healed, and yet we know from experience that very few people are automatically healed the moment they become Christians. They have to *appropriate* healing by either believing for it, releasing faith, standing on the healing scriptures, having someone pray over them for healing, or getting that sickness cast out of them.

The same principle applies to deliverance and breaking of those generational curses. Christ gave his followers the tools and authority to *cast out demons*. It's not an automatic thing—they don't automatically leave the moment you become a Christian. That would be nice, but it's just not that easy. It requires believers to do some warfare, and that's how we partner with God.

The Root and the Fruit

You have no idea how many Christians tell me, "I can't believe I finally found the kind of help I really needed." Sadly in the Christian world, when we have problems, we'll hear, "Brother, you need to crucify the flesh." Well, you can't crucify demons nor can you cast out flesh. It's only after the demons are cast out that we are able to crucify the flesh. So because they can't find the help needed in the church—only counseling is usually offered, which can pinpoint our problems but doesn't get the roots out—they condemn themselves or give up on the Word of God or go to the world for help—like psychiatrists or psychics.

One more word on counseling, while in some cases working through and talking through problems may be effective, you never see Jesus sitting for hours upon hours counseling anyone—but you do see him casting out demons! From my experience counseling is a good tool to pinpoint our problems and find out the root of those problems. However, from that point on, counseling does little good. We can talk about our problems until we are blue in the face, but unless we eradicate the roots—which can only be done through valid inner healing and deliverance—people can go to counseling for years and nothing ever changes! I am in no way trying to diminish the importance of counseling, only making the point that many of our problems have supernatural roots.

Let me give you a word picture of what I'm talking about regarding roots. Let's suppose that you hate apples but you have an apple tree on your property which came with the home you bought. So you go out there and pick all the apples off the tree, hoping they will not grow again next year. But next year at the same time, the apples are there; admittedly, you'd have to be pretty ignorant to think you'd gotten rid of the problem. You go through the same process, only this time you cut back some of the branches hoping the apples will not grow again. But the next year, you get an even bigger crop. Why? Because if you don't want that apple tree to produce apples, you have to pull out the roots. Most counseling goes after the fruit rather than the root. The following case underscores two very important issues which I've just covered: the limitations of counseling and Christians being told they could not possibly have demons.

Dan was referred to me by the pastor of a church we were both attending at the time. He was referred to me as a "last ditch effort." He had counseled with the pastor for years, but nothing seemed to change. When he initially approached me about an appointment, he was very skeptical but said he was desperate enough to try anything to save his marriage.

He told me his wife was filing for divorce because of the emotional abuse he'd subjected her to. Dan was in his mid-forties, a very successful businessman, had a very charismatic personality, and was brilliant; he was also the most intense human being I've ever met. Seemingly, he had everything going for him. He was a very handsome man and loved the Lord. But he admitted that he was emotionally abusive to his wife, and after twenty some years of marriage counseling and nothing changing in him, she'd had enough and wanted out of the marriage. As I listened to his story, I immediately asked him if his parents were emotionally abusive to him when he was a boy, and he said that his dad had been. So we set up an appointment.

When I interviewed him during his first appointment, I also found that he had graduated from Rhema Bible College and that they had been taught that a Christian could not have a demon, so he was skeptical. Because of his desperation, he was willing to try anything. I also found out that being Sicilian, he had mafia in his bloodline, which immediately told me where the violence that he exhibited toward his wife came from.

I started by ministering inner healing to that little boy who had been so verbally abused by his father, and he wept like a baby. After the inner healing, I went for the rejection, abuse, violence, bitterness, hate, self-hate, aggressiveness, rage, anger, control, and much more. The demons, when they were called up, turned him into a five-hundred-pound gorilla. He manifested so strongly that he bent the metal rod under the chair that he was seated on. He came for several more sessions during which I broke all the generational curses operating in his life.

This once extremely intense and aggressive man became a little lamb. His entire personality changed after those demons were cast out. He then confessed that before he found me, he'd been driving down the freeway with a gun on the front seat. He was ready to "blow his brains out" because of his hopelessness and depression. Another life snatched out of the grips of Satan! The greatest thing he said was that he and his wife had tried everything for twenty years, and nothing worked until he came for deliverance. He compared it to having this key ring full of keys, and he'd tried every key and nothing worked until he finally found the right key—deliverance. To God be the glory!

I also had a very sweet, beautiful, elderly lady by the name of Joanne (you can see her testimony on our Web site) call me one day and tell me that she had had a nervous breakdown several years ago, and she was in major depression. She no longer had the will to live. She and her husband spent thousands of dollars on counseling, all to no avail. Well, she started coming to my services where I do teaching and then either take people through individual deliverance or group deliverances. She and her husband attended all the weekly sessions for a month. She, to date, has not as yet had an individual deliverance session, due to the overwhelming demand. However, after simply attending the services and the group deliverances, she got up and gave a testimony. She said that since coming to Isaiah 61, her joy has been restored where before she didn't want to go on living. She said before she started attending the ministry meetings, when she'd go to a funeral, she'd look at the person in the casket and wish it were her. Her life has been totally turned around, and she once again knows the "joy of her salvation."

Her sister called me shortly afterward and told me that this woman's husband had also been completely transformed. She told me that prior to coming to deliverance, he wouldn't even speak to her because she was spirit-filled and operating in the gifts of the Spirit. However, since coming to the deliverance ministry, he now receives her graciously, and his mindset has been changed. She was so delighted in the changes she saw in her family members and went on to say how very much this type of ministry and teaching is needed in the churches.

Demons are trespassers and will continue their unlawful practices until they are confronted. If they are not cast out, they will arrest the spiritual maturity process, bring confusion in the mind, create strongholds, and prevent believers from doing the work of Christ. They will also keep them sick and in poverty so that they stay so focused on their problems that they can never break free to do what Christ has called them to.

SPIRITUAL WARFARE: KNOWING OUR AUTHORITY

"...the kingdom of heaven suffereth violence, and the violent shall take it by force" (Matthew 11:12, KJV).

In this chapter I am going to deal with spiritual warfare that is needed to take back our nation for the Lord and how to overcome attacks from Satan's headquarters against us and our loved ones, i.e. learning to do spiritual warfare through knowing our authority in Christ. This has little to do with individual deliverance needs. It is, however, through learning our authority and learning to do spiritual warfare that we can receive great anointing in the area of deliverance of individuals. First we must learn to become warriors, and that comes through engaging in many battles with the enemy of our souls/nation.

God has chosen mankind to do his work on this earth—spread the gospel, heal the sick, and cast out demons, i.e. to establish His kingdom on this earth and in people's lives.

Psalm 115:16 says, "The heavens, even the highest heavens belong to God, but the earth He has given to mankind." So if we don't do our part, and we fumble the ball, it doesn't get done. It's all part of our partnership with God. He will seldom move in circumstances, governments, or nations without first putting it on the heart of believers to intercede and do battle in those circumstances.

Jesus Christ has deputized us to contend with the forces of darkness and take back what belongs both to us and to our nation. Through His finished work at the cross, He's given us all authority: "Behold I give unto you power to tread on serpents and scorpions and over all the power of the enemy: and nothing shall by any means hurt you" (Luke 10:19, KJV). His work is finished, and He's now seated at the right hand of the Father.

In his most excellent book *Destined to Overcome*, Paul Billheimer depicts Satan's complete defeat by the death and resurrection of Jesus. He states that "The death of Jesus without his failing in one of the smallest details resulted not only in defeating Satan's purpose to obtain a claim upon Jesus, but it also cancelled all of Satan's claims upon the earth and the entire human race." He also goes on to say, "The fact that Satan seems to be having his way is no reflection upon the genuineness of Christ's victory over Satan at the cross. It means only that the enforcement agency has failed."

Because the body of Christ has not recognized the totality of Satan's defeat, we've been fearful of taking a stand against Satan and his hordes of hell and thus have not been the enforcement agency, the soldiers of the cross, that Christ calls us to be!

Despite the fact that Satan's been completely defeated at the cross of Calvary, he still carries on guerilla warfare with his forces of darkness. God has allowed this, as I mentioned earlier, in order to teach the body of Christ to become overcomers and to train us for reigning with him.

The only way his demons can come into your life is if you, through ignorance, allow them in or as I pointed out earlier, if he has a legal right to harass you in a certain area due to generational sin that's not been dealt with or if you open a door for him through engaging in sin. aside from coming into you, which can only be dealt with through deliverance, Satan and his hordes of hell never stop strategizing and plotting on how to block our walk with the Lord and harass us in every area of our life and prevent us from being effectively used by Christ; his strategy is to keep us focused on our problems.

When we, through ignorance, cry out and say, "Lord, look at what the devil is doing to my loved ones or to this nation. Please do something," He's up there saying, "But I've given *you* my authority and all power over the forces of darkness. Now go to battle with those powers of darkness and take back what they're unlawfully holding in captivity."

We are God's representatives on planet earth. Look at Psalm 115:16! We are His hands, His feet, His voice, and when He wants something done on the earth He's given to us, He'll get someone who knows their authority to pray. Sadly enough, most Christians' total concept of prayer is asking the Father or Jesus Christ to do the very things He's expecting us to do.

Intercession is prayer directed to the Father in Jesus's name. Warfare is directed to Satan and his hordes of hell. Despite Satan's complete and total defeat at the cross of Calvary, most Christians pray as if Christ had not given us complete and total victory.

Spiritual warfare is wrestling with the forces of darkness. What we need to remember is that we are wrestling or battling from a position of victory. Spiritual warfare is simply enforcing the victory of Calvary. As R. Arthur Mathews said, "Victory is an accomplished fact, but it does need a man to lay hold of that victory and precipitate a confrontation with the enemy."

Remember what the Apostle Paul said, "We wrestle not against flesh and blood, but rather against principalities, against powers, against the rulers of the darkness of this world, against spiritual wickedness in high places" (Ephesians 6:12, KJV).

What that scripture is telling us is since Satan does not have a fleshly body, we cannot use fleshly weapons against him, i.e. he cannot be attacked physically. We battle him with our words, in the form of a verbal assault, using the Word of God (the sword of the Spirit), and telling him, "I overcome you Satan by the blood of the Lamb and the word of my testimony. Satan it is written..." He has to back away! "For the weapons of our warfare are not carnal but mighty through God to the pulling down of strongholds" (2 Corinthians 10:4, KJV).

Spiritual warfare is being on the offensive. We must aggressively deal with the powers of darkness when we see them arising against us, our families, and our nation. Satan has lulled the church into a slumber and into deception, believing that nothing happens on this earth that God does not allow.

The Bible warns us that in the end times great darkness will come upon the earth. From what I'm seeing happening in our nation, it seems that every demon from hell has been loosed. Therefore it is imperative that the body of Christ learn spiritual warfare so that we can be victorious over the enemy. This is not an option, but an absolute necessity. God wants to raise up warriors who will rise up against the forces of darkness and contend with the enemy.

Jack Hayford in his book *Prayer is Invading the Impossible* said:

> To see both sides of Jesus is to see both sides of prayer. There is the need for compassion, for care, for weeping, for groaning, for aching deeply because of what you sense transpiring in human lives. And it is to learn the place

and time for anger, when we see Satan's wiles successfully destroying; for indignation, when the adversary's program violates territory that is rightfully Christ's; for boldness when demonic hordes announce their presence; for attack, when the Holy Spirit prompts the advance.

Man was made for authority. He was created and fashioned for dominion. God gave mankind dominion over the entire earth to do with as he pleased. There were no strings attached. "For the gifts and callings of God are without repentance" (Romans 11:29, KJV); "For the gifts and callings of God are irrevocable" (Romans 11:29, NAS). So we see in these scriptures that God never takes back a gift. What mankind did with that dominion and authority over the earth was his responsibility; if mankind messed up, God would not step in and repossess His gift.

Most Christians know the story of Adam's disobedience in the garden and how it separated us from the unity with God that we were created for. Most do not understand how Adam's disobedience affected man's rule over the earth. Most do not comprehend the fullness of what happened in the garden of Eden. When Adam chose to listen to Satan and his wife over God, he also transferred his allegiance from God to Satan. With that came the transference of man's dominion.

Since the rule of the earth was a gift from God to man, man could do whatever he chose with that rule and dominion. Because the dominion of the earth was given to man, it was no longer under God's direct control. Then when he (Adam) gave it to Satan, he became the legal ruler of the earth. That's why Satan is called the "god of this world," and "the prince of this world." Satan tricked Adam and Eve with great subtlety into forfeiting the title for dominion of this earth to him, and curse came upon the earth.

You may be one who believes that because God is sovereign, He could have taken dominion of the earth back from Satan and given it to mankind once again. If God had done that, He would have been violating the laws He set into the universe. God has bound himself to these laws and principles, which He put into the universe.

God's Plan for Recovery: Jesus Christ

The only way God could legally recover the earth for man was through a man, the original trustee of the earth. A man had to be found to remove Satan's legal claim to the earth so it could be restored to its original ruler. Of course, this man would have to be one upon whom Satan had no claim or control—one who was absolutely perfect. He could not be a descendant of Adam's, for then he would be tainted with the sin of Adam.

He had to be fully man to enter into this legal battle and fully God in order to live a perfect life. If Jesus was not the son of Mary and the son of God by virtue of a supernatural conception and if he was the son of Mary and Joseph and inherited Adam's propensity to sin, he would have been disqualified to enter the greatest battle ever fought. The destiny of the entire earth and the human race depended upon the outcome of this battle.

From the Bible accounts, we know that from the moment of His birth at Bethlehem all the way to Calvary, there was a fierce battle waged as Satan tried to have Jesus destroyed before He could accomplish His mission. Failing to destroy him, Satan pulled out all stops to try and get him to sin so he could control Him and remain the undisputed ruler of the earth and the human race. But praise God, "For we do not have a high priest who cannot sympathize with our weaknesses, but one who has been tempted in all things as we are, yet was without sin." (Hebrews 4:15).

We know Jesus remained the perfect Son of Man and the perfect Son of God as he was locked in mortal combat in the fiercest battle ever waged with the fallen "son of the morning," this usurping prince.

At long last, the battle was won! The death of Jesus on the cross, without a single failure in his mission, resulted in the defeat of his claim upon the earth and the entire human race.

Sad to say, most in the church act as if they're not certain if Calvary was a defeat or a victory. There is the lack of understanding of the completeness of the victory; they do not appropriate the authority and dominion that Christ handed to the church. Satan is a master at subterfuge; he uses smoke and mirrors to deceive the body of Christ.

No matter what we see happening around us, we must remember that legally, Calvary was Satan's complete undoing. Christ's finished work at the Cross of Calvary completely destroyed Satan. Satan's legal rights to the earth and mankind were completely cancelled. Like any other legal transaction, Christ's finished work at the cross must be enforced. The enforcement of His victory over Satan was placed in the hands of the church. We are His law enforcement agency. We, who are His corporate body upon the earth, are His hands and feet and voice to enforce the victory.

You can bet that Satan works overtime to keep the full truth of the complete legal victory of the cross of Calvary from the church. He knows that if we realized what actually happened to him at Calvary, if we understood the completeness of his defeat, if we knew the fullness of our authority, we could turn this nation and the world upside down.

Satan knows that if the church came into the full knowledge of how to use the authority that has been delegated to her, he'd be blown out of the water and done for. We must bear in mind at all times that we battle from a position of victory, not defeat.

The battle has already been won. We are only called to enforce that victory in the lives of our loved ones, this nation, and our government. We cannot fall asleep at the switch. We are God's law enforcement agency on this earth!

If you get nothing else out of this book, my prayer is that the eyes of your understanding will be opened, and you will once and for all get it into your spirit the great authority that Christ has handed to us.

The issue of walking in our authority on the earth is often times missing from the body of Christ in our Western culture. Look at what the twelve disciples did after only three short years of being trained up by Jesus—they turned the world upside down. Yet we have people sitting in the church pews who've been believers for years, just getting fed and getting fat spiritually and not doing anything to advance God's kingdom. They are a dam rather than a river.

We don't get saved just to have eternal life and make it to heaven. We get saved to bring others into the kingdom and to do the Lord's work. Much of what we go through in our Christian walk requires spiritual warfare. We are and always will be in a battle with the enemy of our souls until we go home to be with the Lord.

Imagine what would happen if everyone in the Church actually believed the Great Commission and went out there and did great things for God. What if the Church of Jesus Christ learned how to do spiritual warfare and began to contend with Satan and his hordes of hell for the young people of this nation, for the music kingdom, the kingdom of Hollywood, the kingdom of education, the kingdom of television, internet, and worldly governments. God has called the church to be a militant church— one that would establish His will in the earth.

That sure seems like our mandate to contend with Satan for those things that he's stolen from us, both in our personal lives and in this nation as we passively sat by and said, "Oh well, it must be God's will."

There's a school of thought in the church that Satan cannot do anything except what God allows. For those who hold that belief, you need to read what God says in 1 Thessalonians, "For we wanted to come to you—I, Paul, more than once—and yet Satan thwarted us" (1 Thessalonians 2:18, NAS). It clearly tells us in this scripture that Satan hindered Paul. It doesn't say that God changed His mind about where Paul was to go. Satan certainly does a lot of things God doesn't allow him to. For instance, millions of babies are murdered before they have a chance at life. Can you honestly say that God would allow such a thing?

This was what went on with the pagan nations that Israel conquered in the Old Testament. They would offer up human sacrifices to their gods of Molech and others. The human sacrifices were always babies, which they burnt in the fire as an offering to appease their god Molech. This is why God commanded the Israelites to destroy these nations, because of their abominable practices.

What Satan did back then, he's still doing today in our nation. Only now it's called abortion, and it's supposedly a woman's right. So we see that Satan does a lot of things that God does not allow. Why? Because the church of Jesus Christ has not arisen in their God-given authority and gone to battle against the forces of darkness behind these things.

"For the weapons of our warfare are not carnal, but mighty to the pulling down of strongholds" (2 Corinthians 10:4, KJV). "This charge I commit unto thee, son Timothy, according to the prophecies which went before thee, that thou by them mightest war a good warfare" (1 Timothy 1:18, KJV). These scriptures tell us we are in a very real war.

Victories are always won in the spiritual realm first, and *then* and only *then* do we see the manifestation of those victories in the natural realm. We do not always see the manifestation of the victory immediately, although sometimes it is immediate. See it we will!

A few more scriptures that confirm that we are in a battle and that we are to be the army of the Lord Jesus Christ—that we are soldiers in a war: "Your troops will be willing on your day of battle" (Psalm 110:3, NIV). "Endure hardship with us like a good soldier of Christ Jesus (2 Timothy 2:3–4, NIV).

Why would the Apostle Paul admonish us to put on the full armor of God if we were not going to be engaged in battle? "Finally, my brethren, be strong in the Lord, and in the power of his might. Put on the whole amour of God, that ye may be able to stand against the wiles of the devil" (Ephesians 6:10–18, KJV). These were all admonitions from the Apostle Paul to let us know that the Christian life is not a pleasure cruise but a battle, and we are the army of God.

All signs seemingly point to the fact that we are living in the end times. We have only to look at what is happening with Israel and the Middle East to see some end time prophecies coming to fruition. When we see the global economic crisis—bear in mind that it's a setup for a one-world government, a one-world currency—just as predicted in the end time scriptures. Satan knows that his time is short, and he's pulling out all stops.

Only those who have buried their head in the sand can be unaware that we are involved in severe warfare for the hearts and minds of the people of our nation. Satan had done his best to lull the church in America to sleep as we've watched the moral decay of our society.

Bob Fraley, in his booklet "A Time For Action," says:

> It's not a matter of enlisting or remaining a civilian. Our Leader hasn't given us that choice. All Christians have already been drafted. There is not a single follower of Christ

who has not been called to become a soldier in God's army: to serve as "Salt and Light." There is no option. We can only be one of three things: a warrior, a deserter, or a POW. Satan delights in deserters and POWs because they support his cause by their inactivity.

Our soldier role is pictured for us throughout the Old and New Testaments. We are not to seek détente with Satan. We must be on the offensive against Satan and his strategies at all times rather the defensive. We must walk in great discernment in order to be able to recognize the schemes and strategies of Satan.

It is imperative that the church of Jesus Christ arise and become what God has ordained us to be—a strong army of mighty warriors.

As I stated before, everything in this world is first accomplished in the spirit realm. Then we see the manifestation of it in the natural, but someone has to rise up and take their God-given authority and take it back. Didn't God say, "I sought for a man who would...stand in the gap...but found no one" (Ezekiel 22:30, NKJV)? In Psalms, God asks, "Who will rise up for me against the wicked? Who will take a stand for me against evildoers" (Psalm 94:16, NIV)? I don't know about you, but something within me screams out, "Me, Lord! I will be that one!"

The book of Ephesians says, "... and raised us up with Him, and seated us with Him in Heavenly places" (Ephesians 2:6, NAS). In the first chapter of Ephesians, it talks about Christ being raised from the dead and being seated at the right hand of the Father "far above all principality and power and might and dominion, and every name that is named, not only in this age but also in that which is to come. And He put *all things* under His feet..." (Ephesians 1:20–22, NKJV). Therefore, since *we're* seated together with Christ in heavenly places, they're—

all principalities, powers, might, and dominion—under *our* feet. we act like we have no power or authority!

Now a word of caution for anyone who would be new at spiritual warfare: If you're going to go against kingdoms of darkness, always pray with at least one other person. Jesus always sent out his disciples in pairs, never alone. Cover yourselves, your loved ones, your possessions, and your animals in the blood of Jesus. Bind (according to Matthew 18:18) and forbid retaliation, retribution, revenge, ambush, and sabotage against yourselves, your loved ones, your possessions, and your animals before you start and at the end of your session. I guarantee that you will not be attacked. God's Word tells us that "One man of you shall put to flight a thousand" (Joshua 23:10, Amplified Bible). The book of Matthew states, "Again I say unto you, that if two of you shall agree on earth as touching anything that they shall ask, it shall be done for them of my Father which is in heaven" (Matthew 18:19, KJV).

Also, it is important to bind the powers of the air over the place where you're gathering for praying and send confusion into the demonic realm. It prevents confusion in your warfare. Satan places ruling spirits over areas, churches, ministries, businesses, neighborhoods, families, and individuals. If you do not bind (according to Matthew 18:18) those ruling spirits, you will not have good success in your warfare, and the following two true stories will demonstrate this t.

Dr. Paul Yonggi Cho says that revival came to South Korea after they bound up the strongman over South Korea. In his book *Spiritual Warfare*, Richard Ing tells the story of a missionary who was passing out Bible tracts in a town where the main street was the border between Paraguay and Brazil. When he was on the Brazilian side of the street, people accepted the tracts and listened to the Word willingly. When he crossed over to the Paraguayan side, people were hostile and unwilling to listen. Amazingly, he tried to approach one woman in Paraguay, and she adamantly refused to listen or even accept a tract. When she crossed over to the Brazil side, the missionary followed her. He offered her the same tract, which she then willingly received and listened to him preach the Word of God to her. Later on, the missionary learned that the churches in Brazil had been praying and binding up the stronghold over their area, but the churches in Paraguay had not. The main street just happened to be the line between principalities.

The trumpet is sounding at the four corners of this nation for the warriors to arise! I pray this will stir you up to want to be used of God as his weapon of war. I have seen dramatic answers to things that my team of warriors and I have gone to battle over.

However, another word of caution here: I have had various people I've talked to reveal that they were pulling down principalities over areas and cities by themselves, without properly covering themselves and their loved ones. My dear friends, that is presumption! You should never attempt those types of things by yourself. You must first of all be sure that God has given you instruction to do that. Then, if that is the case, you must always do that type of thing with other seasoned warriors. It must be at least two or three in agreement. It is a safety net that God has provided for us.

> Again I say to you, that if two of you agree on earth about anything that they may ask, it shall be done for them by my Father who is in heaven. For where two or three have gathered together in my name there I am in their midst.
>
> Matthew 18:19–20

HEAVEN OR HELL

Satan has a well-organized army that plots and strategizes day and night against mankind, especially God's people. He knows his time is short, and he wants to take as many with him to hell as he can to spend an eternity being denied the presence of God, "where the flame dies not and the smoke ever rises." Ever since he rebelled against God and got kicked out of heaven, Satan has been trying to oppose God's agenda for mankind. He knows that there is no redemption for him and the other fallen angels he took with him. Their fate is sealed. He cannot get back at God any other way than to destroy God's beloved creatures, us, who were made in the image of God. So when he takes a person down a pathway of destruction, causing them to either commit suicide or commit murder so they are then executed in a gas chamber or any other act of self-destruction, he celebrates.

Also, every time he gets a human being to reject Jesus Christ, he knows that person's fate is sealed, and he can then populate hell with another soul. By so doing he pokes a finger in God's eye, for he knows that God is grieved over every lost soul. God never created hell for humans to go there, but for Satan and his evil hordes. Unfortunately, those that reject

Christ will spend eternity in the unspeakable horrors of hell. God's Word is very clear on that subject.

There are testimonies of people who've experienced going to hell so that they would come back and tell others of the unspeakable horrors that await those who reject Jesus Christ. It is a place of such extreme heat—fire all around that never goes out—unspeakable thirst, and unspeakable torment, as the demons torture and torment every soul who ends up there.

One man, Bill Wiese, who has written a book entitled 23 *Minutes in Hell* and also has a CD out on his experience of going to hell, says that it took him a full year to get over the horrors of what he saw. The one thing he'll never forget is the intense hatred that demons have for mankind. He did not go there because he was in rebellion against God but as an "on-fire-for-God Christian." God knew he could be trusted to come back and "sound the trumpet" so that all would know what awaits them if they reject Jesus Christ.

For those reading this book who do not know Jesus Christ as Lord and Savior, I would invite you in this very moment to utter these words and mean them:

> Jesus, I confess that I am a sinner, and I ask you to forgive me of my sins. I believe you are the Son of God and that you died on the cross for my sins. I ask you right now to come into my heart and be my Lord and Savior and help me to live the rest of my life for you.

If you've said those words and meant them, it is done. You will spend eternity with Jesus Christ in heaven. There are other steps you must take: get yourself a Bible, find yourself a good Bible-teaching and Bible-believing church, and begin your spiritual journey.

You are now born again. In other words, your spirit has been reborn into God's kingdom and God's ways. Obviously, you were not physically born again. We are born physically one time, and the second birth or the being born again is a spiritual birth. Our spirits that were once separated from God are now joined with Him. Jesus said, "Verily, verily, I say unto thee, except a man be born again, he cannot enter into the kingdom of God" (John 3:3, KJV). Everything that was lost when Adam sinned, Jesus, the second Adam, came to get back for us. Now we must simply appropriate his promises.

There is a great lie being propagated by Satan through the New Age movement, and that is that there are many different ways to heaven. Dear reader, do not swallow that lie. There is one way and one way alone, and it is through Jesus Christ. The Bible tells us that the only way to the Father is through the Son. Jesus said, "Enter through the narrow gate. For wide is the gate and broad is the road that leads to destruction and many enter through it. But small is the gate and narrow the road that leads to life, and only a few find it" (Matthew 7:13, NIV). He was speaking of the way to heaven. Again Jesus said, "I am the *way* and the *truth* and the *life*. No one comes to the Father except through me" (John 14:6, NIV) (Italics mine). We can only get to heaven through Jesus Christ.

A BLESSED LAND

"Blessed is the nation whose God is
the Lord" (Psalm 33:12, NIV)

To the reader who currently is or has in the past been involved in the New Age movement, let me give you a very brief understanding of the danger. New Age is a religion based primarily on Hinduism and other Eastern mystical ideas. These are religions whose followers worship hundreds of demon gods. To see the reality of the curse that this type of worship brings on individuals and nations, visit India or Haiti. Take a look at the fruit of that type of worship! These are perfect examples of cursed nations. They are the most impoverished nations on the face of the earth.

The New Age movement seeks to bring this to America, which has been the most prosperous and blessed nation on the face of the earth. Our forefathers came to America seeking God and a godly freedom, and the result was a blessed nation. The pilgrims bowed their knee at Plymouth Rock and dedicated this America to the Lord Jesus Christ. If you read documents from our founding fathers, you will see that all of those documents included scriptures and prayer. This nation was founded upon God and godly principles. The only way to receive the blessings of God is according to Matthew 6:33 to seek *Him* first, and then He adds unto us His blessings. God promises blessings to those who call him Lord and Savior and to nations who put their trust in Him: "Blessed is the nation whose God is the Lord" (Psalm 33:12, NIV).

There are many books available that will bear out the reality of the blessings of following Christ and the consequences of following other gods. Many books give data comparing the quality of life in certain nations—ranging from income, health, and longevity—to ability to feed the people, the literacy rate, personal freedom, and other areas.

There is much documented data comparing the quality of life in the Christian nations with that in Islamic, Buddhist, Hindu, tribal-religious, and non-religious countries. The difference is phenomenal. You can see so clearly the benefits of following the right God and living by the Bible, which is what was the norm in America until the last few decades! We have only to look at one simple fact to know that we've been a blessed nation. You don't see anyone crossing borders and trying to sneak into any of the other nations; we only have that problem in America.

Why has our nation prospered so greatly and been blessed above all the other nations on the face of the earth? It's very simple; we have been a Christian nation. That is until recently, as evil forces within our nation have tried to remove every symbol of Christianity from our land. When the courts legislated the removal of prayer from our schools, kids started to bring guns to the schools instead. It is now alright for our schools to teach courses on witchcraft and Hinduism and every other sort of occult thing. But mention the name of Jesus? Halloween is a "holiday" celebrated with great fanfare in all the public schools, yet one cannot even say "Merry Christmas" any more without opposition!

Prior to the counterculture revolution in the 1960s, the greatest problem in the public schools were kids being disciplined for chewing gum. Slowly, thanks to the likes of Anti-Christ organizations like the ACLU (American Civil Liberties Union) and Madelyn Murray O'Hare, all symbols of our Christian heritage are being removed from our culture, under the guise of constitutional separation of church and state. For those who are uninformed, that sounds good; however, upon reading the Constitution, you will find that the only thing the Constitution forbids is a state religion.

The First Amendment of the Constitution is clear: "There is to be no federal law respecting an establishment of religion or prohibiting the free exercise thereof." The founding fathers of this nation wanted to prohibit the creation of a national church. It was never their intent to mute Christianity. There is *no constitutional mandate for separation of church and state.* The state does not need to be "protected" from the church. If anything, the church now needs to be protected from the state!

Reverence for God, so evident throughout so much of our history as a nation, has been quietly and tragically withdrawn. As a result, the moral compass of the Scriptures has been set aside in America. Public morality has dangerously declined to unprecedented lows. Secular humanism has taken over, and without the moral compass of God's Word, each man does what he thinks is right. This nation, which was once the greatest exporter of the gospel, has now become the greatest exporter of pornography. We have lost our moral compass, and America is suffering.

Since there is no neutral ground—no gray area—in the spirit realm, when light is removed (the Bible tells us that Jesus Christ is the light of the world), darkness takes over. What do we have now in our nation? More violence, rebellion, drug addiction, murder of innocent children, child abuse, profanity, sexual perversion, pedophilia, and pornography than this nation has ever known!

Our jails are filled to overflowing. Why? We have eliminated God from our culture, and we have allowed Satan and his forces of darkness to take over our culture and our young people. You have only to listen to some of the songs our young people are putting into their souls to begin to understand why they are bringing guns to school and committing suicide at an unprecedented rate. Remember Lucifer was the great worship leader until his pride and rebellion got him kicked out of heaven! It only makes sense he would go for the arts and the music as a doorway into culture. Jesus Christ tells us, "The thief comes only to steal, kill and destroy; I came that they might have life, and might have it abundantly" (John 10:10, NAS). One of the names given to Satan in the Bible is "Thief."

ANGELS AND DEMONS

In this chapter, we will be looking at Satan's kingdom and the demonic realm and how they strategize against us. Before we do that, let's look at angels—God's good angels and Satan's fallen angels.

The Bible mentions angels at least three hundred times. The word *angel* means "messenger." Angels are created spirit-beings, divided into three categories: cherubim, seraphim, and archangels. When God created these spirit-beings, He created them perfectly and without sin but with a free will. We'll look at the result of that free will with one of God's chief angels, Lucifer, in a little bit.

It seems from the biblical account in Job 38:4–7 that the angels were created some time before God created the physical universe. "Where were you when I laid the earth's foundation? Tell me, if you understand. Who marked off its dimensions? Surely you know! On what were its footings set, or who laid its cornerstone while the morning stars sang together and all the angels shouted for joy?" (Job 38:4–7, NIV). This was a passage of scripture wherein God was challenging Job with his lack of understanding of the greatness of his God.

We can deduce from the biblical accounts of angels that God created angels and designed and empowered them to assist Him, as their Creator, in carrying out His orders in the world. Also, some of the angelic beings were created with the express purpose of worshipping God around His throne. No one can say with certainty how many of these powerful spirit beings there really are. However, we see in the book of Matthew that Jesus announced, as they came to arrest him, "Do you think I cannot call on my Father, and he will at once put at my disposal more than twelve legions of angels? But how, then would the Scriptures be fulfilled that say it must happen in this way?" (Matthew 26:53, NIV). In those days a legion numbered some six thousand men, so Jesus was talking about tens of thousands of angels.

We also see in Jude 14 throngs of angels accompanying the second coming of the Lord, "See, the Lord is coming with thousands upon thousands of his holy ones … " (Jude 14, NIV). We also see that the Apostle John had a vision of God's throne surrounded with myriads of myriads and thousands upon thousands of angels.

The Bible accounts show us that angels have been given names; although there are only three names of angels revealed: Lucifer, Michael, and Gabriel. Let's look at Michael and Gabriel and see what their particular function and jobs are. Gabriel seems to be God's chief messenger angel. He is shown in four different accounts as bringing messages to God's people. Michael seems to be a chief warrior angel, as evidenced by five different biblical accounts. The most well known account is shown in the book of Daniel. In Daniel, the tenth chapter, we see that Daniel was praying and fasting for his people for twenty-one days when Gabriel, God's messenger angel, appeared to him and told him that his prayers and fast were heard by heaven, and he was there in response to those prayers.

He went on to tell Daniel that the prince (the dark prince or principality) of the Persian kingdom resisted him for twenty-one days. In other words, there was great warfare going on in the heavens. The warfare was too strong for Gabriel, so the account goes on to tell us that Michael, one of God's chief warrior angels, came to help with the warfare and defeated the dark prince over Persia.

This account in Daniel shows us the need to continue to pray and fast until the answers come. It was because of Daniel's persistence in praying and fasting that caused God's messenger to eventually arrive. Answers to our prayers may be hindered by unseen obstacles. Our prayers may be challenged by evil forces, so continue to pray fervently and earnestly. I believe this is the most powerful passage in the Bible showing us the reality of the invisible warfare that goes on at all times over our lives.

God's angels are huge spirit beings. If you look at Revelation 10:1–3, an angel stood with one leg on the earth and one on the sea. In 2 Kings 19:35, one angel destroyed 188,000 Assyrians. Angels are very large and very powerful. Angels have bodies and can materialize as fleshly beings:

> The two angels arrived at Sodom in the evening, and Lot was sitting in the gateway of the city. When he saw them, he got up to meet them and bowed down with his face to the ground. "My Lords," he said, "please turn aside to your servant's house. You can wash your feet and spend the night and then go on your way early in the morning."
>
> Genesis 19:1–2 (NIV)

"Then the woman went to her husband and told him, 'A man of God came to me. He looked like an angel of God, very awesome. I didn't ask him where he came from and he didn't tell me his name" (Judges 13:6, NIV). In the book of Hebrews it says,

"Do not forget to entertain strangers, for by so doing some people have entertained angels without knowing it" (13:2, NIV). We see throughout the Old Testament God's angels appearing to speak to God's people. Oftentimes the angels appear as men. Other times they just appear as angels.

Whenever an angel appeared to anyone in the Bible, their presence was so awesome that the person would fall on his face. The angel would many times preface whatever message was being brought from God with the statement "Fear not!" It's no wonder. They are huge, brilliant, and fearful to behold. If you ever saw an angel, your body might not be able to withstand the angelic presence. We see in Daniel 8:15–19, when the angel Gabriel appeared to Daniel, he was so overwhelmed and actually terrified with the glorious presence of this majestic angel that all the strength left his body. He fell to the ground as one dead. People faint in the presence of angels because the glory of God is all over them, having come directly from the presence of God. They are beings full of light, and their messages are filled with light because God is light.

In Daniel 10:4–20, another of God's messenger angels appeared to Daniel, but from this account it appears it was not Gabriel. Here is the description of the angel who appeared to Daniel:

> I looked up and there before me was a man dressed in linen with a belt of the finest gold around his waist. His body was like chrysolite, his face like lightning, his eyes like flaming torches, his arms and legs like the gleam of burnished bronze, and his voice like the sound of a multitude.
>
> Daniel 10:5–6 (NIV)

For those who don't know what chrysolite is, it is a translucent, semi-precious stone. It goes on to say that Daniel was so overcome with the brilliance of this angel's presence that he, trembling, fell as one dead to the ground. The angel then touched him and said, "Fear not." Some commentators believe that this was an appearance of Christ, while others believe it was an angel because he needed the archangel Michael's help to break through the heavens. I believe it was an angel as no dark prince or dark angel could stop Christ, who is God.

We see that God's angels bring answers to our prayers. God's angels provide protection and deliverance. They are assigned to protect us, intervene on our behalf, and deliver us from dangerous situations. My near death automobile accident was a perfect example of that. I'm sure that most of us have seen angelic intervention in our Christian walk. "Are not all angels ministering spirits sent to serve those who will inherit salvation?" (Hebrews 1:14, NIV). God's angels carry out the orders of their Commander-in-Chief, Jesus Christ.

We see in Genesis 24 that the Lord had spoken to Abraham and told him that he would send his angel before him to get a wife for his son, Isaac, from his own country. We see these invisible heavenly beings intervening on our behalf to fulfill God's plans for our lives. For those who love and serve Christ, there are always angels hard at work behind the scenes, bringing God's plans and purposes into our lives. Unfortunately, Satan has his dark angels and hordes of hell opposing those plans as well.

For those in positions of leadership in God's kingdom, there are many more angels assigned to protect them and intervene on their behalf. Those in positions of leadership in the church or the kingdom of God seem to be the object of special angelic presence. However, that protection and support of God's angels is there *only as they are doing the will of God and not adulterating their calling.* The angelic protection and power will be lifted when that is no longer true in a minister's life.

In the chapter on Involvement in Witchcraft and Its Consequences, I tell the story of a woman who flew in from Oregon to attend one of my deliverance meetings. She sat in the back of the room and took a picture of me as I finished my teaching and was preparing to go into the group deliverance session. When she took the picture to be developed, it showed the entire wall behind me lined with *huge* warrior angels with their swords drawn. I am very careful to walk a holy and obedient walk before the Lord, not only because I don't want to lose that angelic protection, but because I want to be pleasing to my Lord and Savior! It is not a difficult thing to do when you love the Lord. Jesus said in John 14:15, "If you love me, you'll keep my commands"

The Bible shows us that angels also dispense supernatural provision. After Elijah killed 450 of Jezebel's false prophets who worshipped the pagan god Baal, as recorded in 1 Kings 19:1, we see that Elijah then fled into the desert when Jezebel threatened to have him killed. He sat under a broom tree and felt so hopeless that he wanted God to just take him home. Anybody identify with that? Usually after great spiritual victories, there are great spiritual attacks. Well, what did God do instead? He sent an angel who prepared food for him and gave him instructions on what to do next. So the angel not only provided sustenance for his body but comfort for his soul.

We know from the Word of God and history that angels, both good and bad, influence government, economics, culture, and work behind the scenes to shape history. When God's people get to praying and warring for righteousness to prevail in their government, their culture, and their nation, they release God's plans into a nation. When God's people neglect their responsibility to pray and do warfare over God's plans and purposes for their nation, Satan's dark angels gain ground.

The book of Revelation gives us clear insight into the fact that angels are involved in natural disasters. Sometimes it is God's angels bringing judgment, and other times it is Satan's dark angels wanting to destroy. I will give you an example of that in a minute. In the book of Revelation, which is a book about the end times, we see that God's angels are given power over the weather; they are commanded to "hold back the four winds of the earth to prevent any wind from blowing on the land or on the sea or on any tree" (Revelation 7:1, NIV). Also in Revelation we see "the seventh angel poured out his bowl into the air ... and there came flashes of lightning, peals of thunder and a severe earthquake" (Revelation 16:17–18, NIV). These scriptures also confirm for us that God's angels play a major role in carrying out the judgments of God, most significantly in the last days. God is the judge and his angels are administrators of God's justice. Yes, God is a God of love, but Psalm 97:2 tells us that his throne is founded upon two pillars—righteousness and justice. He is patient and long-suffering; however, when individuals or nations choose to continue in their sinful, rebellious ways, then they bring judgment upon themselves.

We also know that there are angels of death who appear to take God's people to their eternal home in heaven. We see that angels are God's helpers in administering all of God's commands.

The following story will bring clear insight into how Satan's dark angels and dark princes also work behind the scenes, but with one purpose alone—to bring destruction:

I remember reading and hearing many years ago that Peter Wagner was preparing to take a group of spiritual warriors and intercessors to Turkey to pull down "Diana," the principality over Turkey, and to open the heavens for the Spirit of God to be released into that country. To the best of my recollection, they had a group of about 5,000 people signed up to go on that missionary journey. Right before they were to depart, there was a major earthquake in Turkey that killed thousands of people; most were unsaved, I'm sure, as the majority were Muslims. It doesn't take major discernment to see which angels were behind that disaster. Satan knew what was planned and assigned his dark angels to bring that disaster before the people could be saved. His greatest desire is to populate hell with God's beloved creation, mankind! There are dark angels, or territorial spirits, assigned by Satan over nations, cities, communities, governments, and media. We have only to look at the perversion in every form of media, television, radio, music, and movies to know who's controlling these.

Since there is great deception going on in our culture concerning angels, it's important for us to understand what God's angels don't do, so as to not be seduced into what the New Agers are teaching about angels.

Most importantly, God's angels will never receive worship. They know they are simply God's messengers and that all glory belongs to Him. As you look at the Old and New Testament accounts of angelic visitations, you will see that the person being visited would be so overwhelmed with the awesome presence that they fall on their faces to worship the angel. We see in Revelation 19:9 an angel instructing John the Apostle, and it says in Revelation 19:10, "At this I fell at his feet to worship him. But he said to me. 'Do not do it! I am a fellow servant with you and your brothers who holds to the testimony of Jesus. Worship God!'"

The angel would always reach down and bring the person to his feet so that they would not be in a position of worship. The Bible is very clear on that account. We are also never to pray *to* angels. We can ask the Lord to send his angels to encamp around us for protection or ask that they be sent ahead of us into any adverse situation we'll be entering into, to prepare the victory for us. New Age, on the other hand, teaches the worship of angels and that we're to pray to angels.

When you begin to understand the great authority we've been given, and the fact that we're surrounded by armies of heaven at all times, *you* can send the angels into a potentially danger-ous situation or post angels around yourself and your loved ones to protect yourself and them from Satan's plots, schemes, and strategies. Most of our angelic protection goes to waste, as the warrior angels stand with their swords at their sides waiting for orders. Didn't Jesus say "…he who believes in Me, the works that I do he shall do also; and greater works than these shall he do…" (John 14:12, NAS). He said He could have commanded twelve legions of angels to come to his assistance had he wanted to. Whenever I start my group deliverance meetings, I loose the warring angels to fill up the place and assist in the warfare.

Contrary to what New Age teaches about angels, we can-not send angels to get us a million dollars or to get whatever we want. They are there for our protection and to nudge us into what God has for us. They will not do anything that is not the will of God.

Another difference between what the Bible shows us in regards to angels and what the New Age movement teaches is the fact that nowhere in the Bible do we see people initiating a conversation with an angel. The angels always talk first. The New Age movement, however, encourages relationships with angels the same way you would with a close personal friend. The believer's close friend is the Holy Spirit. He is our coun-selor, our teacher and our instructor, not the angels. Just as God would never violate the free will He's given to man, so it is with His good angels. They will never violate our free will. Although they're assigned to protect us, they cannot come to our aid when we're walking in willful sin, only when we're believing and obeying God.

Also contrary to New Age teaching on angels, God's Word shows us that angels are always male. There are no female angels. Remember that it tells us in Genesis and other books of the Old Testament that angels were called the sons of God.

Last but not least is the fact that angels, unlike God, are not omnipresent (everywhere at once), omnipotent (having infinite power), or omniscient (having infinite knowledge).

Satan, ever the counterfeiter, also has a very highly organized hierarchy of fallen or dark angels and demons. From my study of the Word of God, I understand that Satan's angels are not demons. I believe that the dark angels comprise the principalities, powers, and spiritual wickedness in high places mentioned in Ephesians 6:12, Colossians 1:16 and 2:15. In Acts 23:8–9, Paul seems to distinguish between angels and unclean spirits (demons and evil or unclean spirits appear to mean the same thing to the Gospel writers).

Therefore we can conclude that the fallen angels can and do have bodies and would not seek to inhabit a human body. While demons, being disembodied, constantly seek to inhabit bodies, either human or animal. The Gospel accounts in Matthew 12:43 and Mark 5:1–19 tell us that demons do not have bodies. Demons cannot live out their perversion without being in a human body.

Here's some more interesting, albeit controversial, insight into fallen angels as recorded in the Bible. By and large, it's one of those portions of Scripture that the Body of Christ, for the most part, just skips over. I will give you the facts, and you can decide for yourself. The book of Genesis tells us that there were giants on the face of the earth at that time. The Nephilim, according to Genesis 6:1–2, 4, were the product of fallen angels cohabiting with the daughters of men.

And it came to pass, when men began to multiply on the face of the earth, and daughters were born unto them, that the sons of God saw the daughters of men that they were fair; and they took them wives of all which they chose... There were giants in the earth in those days; and also after that, when the sons of God came in unto the daughters of men and they bare children to them, the same became mighty men which were of old, men of renown.

Genesis 6:1–2 and 4 (KJV)

The New American Standard Bible says it this way: "The Nephilim were on the earth in those days, and also afterward, when the sons of God came in to the daughters of men and they bore children to them. Those were the mighty men who were of old, men of renown" (Genesis 6:4, NAS).

It says the sons of God, which in the Old Testament always referred to as angels, not men. Also if "sons of God" are not angels in the Genesis 6 account, why would the book of Jude tell us that sins of those angels who "kept not their first estate" and who are held in everlasting chains until judgment were "fornication" and "going after strange flesh" (Jude 6:7, KJV). The term *sons of God* in Genesis 6:1–2 and 4 is also used in five other passages in the Old Testament. Every single time the expression refers to angels. Grant Jeffrey's book *Unveiling Mysteries of the Bible* tells us that Genesis 6 recounts how the "sons of God," the fallen angels, were a key reason God was forced to destroy the earth with a great flood during the days of Noah. God had determined to destroy the mutant hybrid offspring of this unholy union of angels and the daughters of men.

Jeffrey goes on to say that Satan's apparent purpose in directing this demonic corruption of humanity through these fallen angels was intended to prevent any pure, undefiled genetic human line through which the promised Messiah, Jesus Christ, humanity's only hope of salvation, could be born. Well, guess what? God checkmated Satan again with the flood! Are you getting the picture? Satan's greatest brilliance is no match for God's unfathomable wisdom and knowledge. In fact, it's pure foolishness—the created angel thinking he's smarter than his Creator!

A first century Jewish historian, Josephus, in his book *The Works of Josephus* also addresses the subject of fallen angels cohabiting with women. He says, "For many angels of God accompanied with women, and begat sons that proved unjust, and despisers of all that was good, on account of the confidence they had in their own strength; for the tradition is, that these men did what resembled the acts of those whom the Grecians called giants."

Yes, Jesus did say that angels neither marry nor are given in marriage in Matthew 22:30 and Mark 12:25. However, he is talking about not marrying or being given in marriage in *heaven*. For the dark angels on this earth, it was a different story. Just as God's good angels can appear in the flesh to someone to rescue them in a life or death situation, so Satan's dark angels can materialize in the flesh.

The term *sons of God* was accepted by ancient Jewish synagogues, the Jews of Jesus's time, and also by the early Christian church as referring to fallen angels until the fourth century. Then it was once again believed during the time of the reformation.

Now, let's take a look at demons who are Satan's foot soldiers. There are different theological arguments as to the origin of demons.

The three theories I've heard as to the origin of demons are:

1. They are Satan's fallen angels.

2. They are disembodied evil spirits from a pre-Adamic race.

3. They are the disembodied evil spirits of the civilization that God destroyed in Noah's time.

I personally believe from my study of the Bible and some of the ancient Jewish texts that demons are disembodied spirits from another civilization that was destroyed by God. It may have been when God destroyed the entire civilization that was on the earth in Noah's time or from a civilization that existed prior to Adam and Eve. It tells us in Genesis that God told Adam and Eve to replenish the earth. Replenish speaks of replacing that which once existed. The existence of a pre-Adamic race is suggested by Genesis 1:28 (KJV):

> So God created man in his own image, in the image of God created he him,; male and female created he them. And God blessed them, and God said unto them, Be fruitful and multiply and replenish the earth....

Isaiah 24:1 and Jeremiah 4:23 give us a full description of the earth under curse. Psalm 104:5–9 speaks of God sending a flood on the earth after its original creation.

The KJV version of the Bible, although extremely difficult to understand because of the antiquated language, is the most accurate translation when you want to do a study on these issues. The other translations have changed the original meanings of some of these scriptures. Although I prefer to spend my personal Bible reading time in some of the easier translations, for study purposes, I will check it out against the King James Version.

The theory that seems the most credible to me is that they are disembodied spirits from the wicked civilization which God destroyed in Noah's time, although Scripture does not provide sufficient evidence to prove any of these theories. Dr. Ed Murphy in his book *The Handbook for Spiritual Warfare* says:

Human civilization in Noah's day reached a state of total depravity never known before and never known since. All men in all cultures have become like the future cities of Sodom and Gomorrah. God cannot find even ten righteous men to cause him to hold back the total, universal destruction of the human race. He found only eight in Noah's family: Noah, his wife, three sons, and three daughters-in-law (Genesis 7:1, 7).

Regardless of what the true origin of demons is, we do know that Scripture makes it reasonably clear that demons are not fallen angels since angels have bodies according to Genesis 6:4, and Jude 6:7. Demons do not—they are disembodied spirits with an intense craving to enter a body as we see in Matthew 12:43–45 and Luke 11:24–26.

When we study the Gospel accounts we see that demons are living, functioning, spiritual beings with a mind, personality, and will of their own completely dedicated to the service of Satan. We see that Jesus always treated them as living entities that were diametrically opposed to God's work and committed to the destruction of mankind.

If we study the Gadarean demonic incident as recorded in Mark 5:1–10 and Luke 4:33, we will see that Jesus showed us quite a lot about the spirit realm and unclean spirits.

> They went across the lake to the region of the Gerasenes (some manuscripts say Gadarenes). When Jesus got out of the boat, a man with an evil spirit came from the tombs to meet him. This man lived in the tombs and no one could bind him anymore, not even with a chain. For he had often been chained hand and foot, but he tore the chains apart and broke the irons on his feet. No one was strong enough to subdue him. Night and day among the tombs and in the hills he would cry out and cut himself with stones.

When he saw Jesus from a distance, he ran and fell on his knees in front of him. He shouted at the top of his voice, "What do you want with me, Jesus, Son of the Most High God? Swear to God that you won't torture me?" For Jesus had said to him, "Come out of this man, you evil spirit!"

Then Jesus asked him, "What is your name?"

"My name is Legion," he replied, "for we are many." And he begged Jesus again and again not to send them out of the region."

Mark 5:1–10 (NIV)

Luke 4:33, "And there was a man in the synagogue possessed by the spirit of an unclean demon, and he cried out with a loud voice, 'Ha! What do we have to do with you, Jesus of Nazareth? Have you come to destroy us? I know who you are—the Holy One of God'" (Luke 4:33, NAS). You will notice that the man was in the synagogue. Only God's Covenant people were allowed into the synagogue. This is yet another scripture that shows us that there can be demons in believers or covenant people.

The word "possessed" in this translation has caused much confusion and is due to weaknesses in the way different English versions have translated certain expressions from the original Greek text, which have obscured the meaning for English readers. Since I am not a Greek scholar, I will give you the proper translation from others who are, mainly Derek Prince. The Greek noun *daimon* gives rise to a verb *daimonizo*, which occurs about twelve times in the New Testament. The English equivalent of this verb is *demonize*, which the Collins English Dictionary defines as "to subject to demonic influence." The New Testament shows this verb occurring only in the passive form "to be demonized." However in the original KJB, it's translated as "to be possessed of a devil or devils." The modern versions have correctly changed devil to demon, but incorrectly retain the form "to be possessed."

As I explain in the chapter "Can a Christian Have a Demon?" possession implies ownership, but once a person becomes a Christian, the ownership of his life belongs to His Lord and Savior, Jesus Christ. There is no basis for this in the Greek word *daimonizo*, which means merely "to subject to demonic influence" and contains no suggestion of ownership.

What do we learn from these scriptures? When we look at the Gadarene demoniac account, we see that:

1. Satan's hordes are almost countless; a legion represented anywhere from 4,200 to 6,000 soldiers.

2. Many demons can inhabit a human body.

3. Demons can cause a person to have superhuman physical strength.

4. Demons can talk back and resist being cast out.

5. Demons have intelligence; they tried to bargain with Jesus as to where they would be sent.

6. Demons or unclean spirits desire to be in a fleshly body, preferably a human body, but the second choice is an animal.

7. Demons know the Word of God. The demons knew what the Word says about the end when they will be consigned to the pit (Revelation 20:1, 3). In fact they know the Word of God better than some Christians because they have been around since the advent of time. I have had many a demon speak out and correct a ministry worker if he misquoted Scripture. They'd say, "Ha, that's not what it says, it says thus and such." And they would actually correctly quote the scripture.

8. Demons operate in groups, never singly.

9. Demons oftentimes make people live in foul places and conditions.

The fact that demons can and do speak is shown in many Gospel accounts where Jesus was casting out demons. We see this occurring in Capernaum, at the beginning of Jesus's ministry, where a man stood up in the synagogue and shouted out at Jesus, "What do we have to do with you, Jesus of Nazareth? Have you come to destroy us? I know who you are—the Holy One of God!" (Luke 4:34, NAS). Jesus then expelled or "cast out" that demon from the man, and the crowd was amazed at his authority. In this incident, Jesus commanded the demon to stop speaking. Many use this scripture to say that we shouldn't allow demons to speak or to talk to demons since Jesus didn't. The reason Jesus commanded this demon to "shut up" was because He did not want them to reveal who He really was prematurely. In Mark 1:44 and Luke 9:21, he gave that same order to his disciples. The incident does show us that demons know things human beings don't. They knew He was the Son of God before the people whom He came to save did!

We need to look at full counsel of the Word of God before we make assertions. Mark 5:1–20 and Luke 8:26–39 show us that Jesus carried on a lengthy conversation with the demons in the Gaderene (Gerasene) with one purpose in mind, to set the man free! Not only did he ask the demons their name, but he allowed them to bargain with him.

On the subject of demons knowing things people don't, I'm going to share with you an experience I had many years ago after I first started ministering deliverance. One day a woman, whom I had ministered to previously, called me in a panic. She asked if I could come over to her apartment, as she desperately needed help with a friend who had come from Florida to visit her. She said that all of a sudden the woman just went berserk and locked herself into the bathroom and was screaming and breaking everything in the bathroom, including all the bottles in the medicine cabinet. She was in an absolute panic and didn't know what to do about the friend. As she was telling me about it, I could hear the loud, blood-curdling screams in the background. This woman was afraid she would get kicked out of her apartment.

It was impossible for me to get over to her apartment, so I asked her if she had a speakerphone, which she did. I told her to put it right outside the locked bathroom door. As soon as she did that, I commanded the demon in the woman to tell me its name. As I was speaking, the friend said, "She's got her hand under the bathroom door, trying to grab the phone." I then again commanded the demon to "shut up" and stop the screaming and tell me its name. The screaming stopped immediately, and then in the most hair-raising voice, the demon said, "Eleanor, we *know* you," drawing out the words. It was so eerie sounding that it made the hair on my arms stand up. I responded with "Good, so now tell me your name, you foul spirit!" It did, and I commanded it to renounce its claim to the woman and go to the pit. Immediately she started retching and was back in her right mind. The moral of the story is that this woman did not know my name or who I was as she was from Florida, and her friend had never mentioned me. The demons, however, know those with authority and a calling on their lives, and they spread the word. So even the demons in Florida knew who I was!

It was not always this way. Prior to my being thrust into the ministry of deliverance, I was completely ignorant on the subject of demons and the spiritual realm. Another incident with the demonic had far different results.

One day a neighbor who was from the Ukraine came over and asked if I would come over and pray for her twelve-year-old daughter who was really sick with a high fever and needed help. They were a beautiful family but were in an Orthodox Catholic Church. She knew I was a strong, praying Christian, so she came to me for help.

She took me into the daughter's bedroom and left the room to get me something to drink. I sat on the girl's bed and laid hands on her and started to command the fever to go in Jesus's name. All of a sudden, I heard this deep, deep man's voice speaking out of the girl's mouth, and it said, "*Don't* say that *name!*" The hair stood up on the back of my neck, and I "freaked out." I jumped up in complete fear, left the room quickly, told the mother I'd prayed, excused myself, and went home as fast as my legs could carry me. I didn't know what to make of the incident, until years later. That poor girl needed deliverance, and I wasn't able to help her because I was in total ignorance on the subject of demons as most of the body of Christ still is.

As we saw earlier, demons are living spirit beings with a mind, a will, and personality of their own with intelligence and emotions. They are also completely dedicated to the service of Satan—mostly due to fear. I've cast out many a demon that would cry and whine and say, "Don't send me to the pit, please. You have no idea how terrible it is there." Or they would say, "Oh, oh, I'm in trouble now!" Satan's kingdom is ruled by fear. God's kingdom is ruled by love. Satan's army is well-trained. There is absolutely no love among demons, but they are united in one purpose and one purpose alone. That is the destruction of mankind.

Let's look at the scripture accounts that show us the reality of demons having a mind, will, intelligence, emotions, and a personality

We see in Matthew, Jesus saying:

> When an unclean spirit goes out of a man, it goes through dry places, seeking rest, and finds none. Then he says, I

will return to my house from which I came. And when he comes, he finds it empty, swept and put in order. Then he goes and takes with him seven other spirits more wicked than himself and they enter and dwell there; and the last state of that man is worse than the first.

Matthew 12:43–45 (NKJV)

Now, this scripture account shows us many of things about demons or unclean spirits. It shows us the reality that the demon had the intelligence to think that the place it has just come from might still be empty and desirable to go back to. It shows that it has a will of its own, and demons usually work in groups, very rarely alone.

It also was a warning from Jesus that when we receive deliverance by the casting out of unclean spirits that if we don't fill ourselves up with the things of God then those spirits will return with seven times more, and we will be worse off than before. This is a reality. It is also confirms the fact that deliverance is only for Christians, for what would unbelievers have to keep the unclean spirits from returning?

In James 2:19 it says, "Even the demons believe and tremble" (James 2:19, NKJV)! This scripture shows fear in operation. Fear is an emotion. I personally have ministered to many people who, at the start of the session, would be trembling violently. They thought that it was them trembling, but as the session would progress, they'd see the reality of what was in operation. They would realize that it was the demons that were trembling with fear because they knew their time was up in that vessel. "God has not given us a *spirit of fear*, but of power and love and sound mind" (2 Timothy 1:7, NKJV). Fear is a spirit. James was also making it known that demons know and recognize the truth of God and His Word—not that they trust in God, as believers do.

Though some of the body of Christ doesn't believe that demons exist, the truth is that there is an invisible world that is just as real as the visible world. Not only is there an invisible world, but that world is in a constant state of invisible conflict. Jesus gave us the pattern in the New Testament. He didn't refer to demons in the abstract. They spoke to Him, and He spoke back.

We must remember that the very evidence of those who believe *is signs following them* (Mark 16:17). In Mark 16:17, Jesus tells his disciples that signs shall follow those who believe. That in his name they would drive out demons! These signs include casting out demons! It is imperative to our prosperity that we understand the biblical dynamics of spiritual realities. If we don't, we will be defeated in many areas by these invisible evil spirit beings. We can't see the wind, yet we feel its effects. We can't see bacteria with the naked eye, yet that doesn't make it any less real. We can't see natural gas, yet we use it. So we also need to be aware of the workings of the spirit realm and how it affects our lives on a daily basis.

I'm going to give you some characteristics of demons as revealed by the Bible:

1. They are spirits without bodies (Ephesians 6:12).

2. They are numerous (Mark 5:8–9).

3. They are organized (Matthew 12:24).

4. They have supernatural powers (Revelation 16:14).

5. They are knowledgeable of God (Matthew 8:29).

6. They are in believers and can torment them (Matthew 12:43–45).

7. They are able to inflict sickness and infirmity (Matthew 9:32–33).

8. They can influence or control animals (Mark 5:13).

9. They can influence or control human beings (Luke 8:2).

10. They can cause mental disorders (Mark 5:2–3,5).

11. They know that Jesus Christ is God (Mark 1:23–24).

12. They tremble before God (James 2:19).

13. They are behind false doctrine (1 Timothy 4:1).

14. They oppose God's people (Ephesians 6:12).

I think it's appropriate that I also give you some of the names of Satan, as revealed in the Bible. His names indicate his nature and his function. Before I do that, I must point out that before he was kicked out of heaven his name was Lucifer. Upon his expulsion from heaven, he was given the name Satan, which means adversary, hater, opponent, and enemy.

Let's look at what Scripture reveals concerning Lucifer before his rebellion against God and what caused him to rebel.

Lucifer means "day star, light bearer, or son of the morning." He was the archangel who was the worship leader in heaven. Ezekiel 28:12–17 gives us a glimpse of Lucifer's role and beauty in heaven—before his arrogance, rebellion, and self-exaltation brought judgment upon him and a swift expulsion from heaven. Although the passages in Ezekiel 28:12–17 seem to be given to the kings of Babylon and Tyre, as prophetic messages often do, there is a dual message. It appears to completely describe what went on in the heavens when Lucifer (Satan) opposed God. This also seems to be the consensus of most biblical scholars.

> You were the model of perfection, full of wisdom and perfect in beauty. You were in Eden, the garden of God; every precious stone adorned you, ruby, topaz and emerald, chrysolite, onyx and jasper, sapphire, turquoise and beryl.

Your settings and mountings were made of gold; on the day you were created they were prepared. You were anointed as a guardian cherub, for so I ordained you. You were on the holy mount of God; you walked among the fiery stones. You were blameless in your ways from the day you were created till wickedness was found in you. So I drove you in disgrace from the mount of God, and I expelled you, O guardian cherub from among the fiery stones. Your heart became proud on account of your beauty and you corrupted your wisdom because of your splendor. So I threw you to the earth.

Ezekiel 28:12–17 (NIV)

The King James Version of Ezekiel says:

Thou hast been in Eden the garden of God; every precious stone was thy covering, the sardius, topaz, and the diamond, the beryl, the onyx, and the jasper, the sapphire, the emerald, and the carbuncle, and gold; the workmanship of thy *tabrets* and of thy *pipes* was prepared for thee in the day that thou wast created.

Ezekiel 28:13 (KJV)

A tabret was a musical instrument used by the prophets in 1 Samuel 10:5 and by the people in Genesis 31:27. Another name for a tabret was a timbrel. The word *pipes* in that version of the scripture also meant a musical instrument. It literally is another word for flute. The King James Version of that scripture gives us the understanding that Lucifer was created with these musical instruments in him with the express purpose of leading the worship of heaven. That is why the fallen angel, Lucifer, corrupts the music of earth. He is behind all the perverse music that is corrupting this younger generation and leading them away from God.

We see from these scripture accounts that Lucifer became lifted up in pride because of his beauty and God-given wisdom and thought he was smarter and greater than his Creator. He became very arrogant and self-exalting and thought he'd become greater than God, which led him to rebel against God. Know anybody like that? I know a lot of people who use their God-given intellect, beauty, and abilities in a corrupt manner, having no need for God and certainly never giving these talents back to God to use for His glory. We have only to look at Hollywood to see the perversion of God-given abilities, beauty, and talent. Rather than realizing that anything they have is only by the Grace of God, they choose to serve Satan with what God has given them, to their demise and destruction.

I have also seen that spirit of pride that was in Satan operating in some churches, trying to cause church splits—one person exalting himself above God's appointed head, the pastor. Now we know that the Bible tells us there are not only false sheep but also false shepherds, so we have to be very discerning in this. I am speaking of God's truly appointed, truly anointed shepherds, not the false ones! Derek Prince says that he saw a lot of churches destroyed by "demons, oh, excuse me, I meant deacons."

We see that Lucifer quickly came under God's judgment and found out he was *only a created being* and certainly no match for the God of the universe. In Luke 10:18 Jesus gives us another glimpse into what happened. Jesus said, "I was watching Satan fall from heaven like lightning." Jesus is telling us that He saw it happen when He was still in heaven with the Father, before His earthly mission.

Then Isaiah 14:12–17 gives us a further glimpse of Lucifer/Satan's rebellion against God and expulsion from God's heaven.

> How you have fallen from heaven, O morning star, son of the dawn! You have been cast down to the earth, you who

have weakened the nations! You said in your heart 'I will ascend to heaven; I will raise my throne above the stars of God; I will sit enthroned on the mount of the assembly, on the utmost heights of the sacred mountain. I will ascend above the tops of the clouds; I will make myself like the Most High.

Isaiah 14:12–14 (NIV)

The following is a list of names of Satan as listed in the Bible:

1. Satan (Job 1:6–12)

2. Lucifer (Isaiah 14:12)

3. Roaring Lion (1 Peter 5:8)

4. Thief (John 10:10)

5. Devil (John 8:44)

6. Beelzebub (Matthew 12:24)

7. God of the Age (2 Corinthians 4:4)

8. Ruler of this World (John 14:30)

9. Prince of the Power of the Air (Ephesians 2:2)

10. Belial (2 Corinthians 6:15)

11. The Enemy (Matthew 13:39)

12. The Wicked One (1 John 5:18–19)

13. Angel of Light (2 Corinthians 11:13–15)

14. Antichrist (1 John 4:1–4)

15. Adversary (1 Peter 5:8)

16. Murderer (John 8:44)

17. Liar (John 8:44)

18. Abaddon or Apollyon (Revelation 9:11)

19. Wolf (John 10:12)

20. Fowler (Psalm 91:3)

21. Angel of the Bottomless Pit (Revelation 9:11)

22. Accuser of the brethren (Revelation 12:10)

23. The Wicked One (1 John 5:18–19)

24. The Tempter (1 Thessalonians 3:5)

Are you getting a pretty good picture of the nature and character of Satan? I cannot even begin to imagine how any human being could ever choose to serve Satan whose only agenda is to destroy mankind!

HOW DEMONS WORK AGAINST US

Let's look at the character of demons and how they operate behind the scenes. I would highly recommend *Final Quest* by Rick Joyner. In the book he shares a vision from the Lord, which spanned months, on how the demonic work against us. The Lord showed him what anyone in the deliverance ministry already knows to be fact—demons push, prod, tempt, and entice people to make bad decisions, to gossip, to become involved in strife, etcetera. Their aim is to cripple and destroy as many of God's plans and God's work as possible. It is a very good book, although it only shows how demons work from the outside. We, who are in deliverance, know how demons work from the inside as well.

Demons put thoughts into our minds, although we are responsible for what we do with those thoughts. Billy Graham once said, "You can no more keep Satan from putting thoughts in your mind than you can keep a bird from flying over your head, but you can keep him from building a nest there." Because they study our weaknesses and exploit them, they will tailor the thoughts to our area of vulnerability. These demons have been around since the advent of time, and they know your family tree better than you do. They know the sins and vulnerabilities of each one of your ancestors that have gone before you, and they will do everything in their power to entice and lead you down the same path of sin.

For instance, demons seldom tempt a person in the sexual sin area who is not already vulnerable in that area. Nor are they likely to tempt one who is not vulnerable to alcoholism to drink. They will persist until they succeed in causing that person's failure and destruction. The greater the weakness, the harder demons will work to cause you to sin in that area. They're like sharks that, smelling blood, attack with great ferocity until they've destroyed their victim. That is their job assignment.

Demons are all around us. They study us, observe our weaknesses and piggyback on those weaknesses by setting up situations whereby we will finally give in to them and slip into sin. When we do, it then gives them an open door to come in and set up shop.

Demons are always behind compulsions such as smoking, drugs, alcoholism, compulsive talking, gluttony, sexual perversion, pornography, strife, contention, and others. All of these compulsions then lead to addiction, which is then coupled with enslavement. When addiction takes over, the only answer is deliverance as people seldom have the strength to break the addiction on their own, since they have now become enslaved to and come under a power that is too strong to break with anything but the remedy provided by Jesus, i.e. the casting out of those spirits of addiction. Pornography is probably one of the strongest addictions for men living in this nation, as we are so flooded with images of scantily clad women in the magazines, on TV, the movies, and everywhere you turn.

When people attempt to solve their addictions without deliverance, they will many times trade one addiction for another. Smokers are a perfect example of that. When someone gives up smoking, they usually put on weight almost immediately. Why? They've traded one addiction for another. They've traded cigarettes for gluttony. Most often the addiction is passed down the bloodline, but at other times young people turn to drugs or alcohol as a substitute for the love and companionship their parents were either too busy or too selfish and self-centered to provide. Parents who are emotionally distant and do not demonstrate love to their children do as much damage as the others. We are all born with a deep and innate need and longing for love and acceptance. When that is denied to a child, he will later turn to other things as a substitute.

The demonic realm works behind the scenes in the unseen spirit realm, pushing people to react in dysfunctional ways and then putting guilt upon them. They love it when people are ignorant of their presence and love it even more when people don't believe they even exist and just blame their problems on "natural" causes.

Demons also love to make people doubt God and His Word. Many of the people I've ministered to have said the following things thinking it was their own thoughts: "How could God allow that to happen?" or "If God really is a God of love, how could he let me be born to these parents?" or "God really doesn't love me" or "Can God really forgive me?" Only after receiving deliverance did they realize that those thoughts were not their own, but rather being put into their minds by demons.

One of their favorite tactics is to get people to retain guilt even after they've confessed the sin and been forgiven by God. Many people blame themselves for the abuse they received at the hands of others, despite the fact that they were the victim.

I ministered to a gentleman in his late forties who had a drug problem. He was a very gifted and intelligent man but had become addicted to drugs as a coping mechanism when his wife left him and he lost his business. As I interviewed him prior to starting the deliverance session, he was saying some things that were very blasphemous. He said things like, "I think God is just plain arrogant and boastful, when he says in the Word 'I am the Great I Am'" and other equally blasphemous things.

When I started the deliverance session, I called up a spirit of blasphemy, and it came up cursing God with the foulest expressions. After it was cast out, I realized that it was the demon, speaking through him during the interview that was blaspheming God. Those demons were using one of their many tricks—lying about who God is. A favorite trick of the demonic is deluding people that these thoughts are their own.

Another fact that we must be aware of is that Satan and his hordes of hell celebrate every time God gets blamed for a tragedy or disaster being visited upon humans. It's amazing how many times in ministering to clients I've heard God being blamed for all the bad things in their lives.

Years ago when I had my ministry in a church, a woman came up to me as I was worshipping and asked to speak to me in the hall. We went out, and she proceeded to unload her burden upon me. She told me that her friend, Al, was going to die if I didn't minister to him. She had seen me on a Christian television program talking about deliverance and traced me to the church I was in at that time. She told me that her friend was suicidal, and the psychiatrists had him on all kinds of drugs, which caused him to be bedridden and consequently lose his job. She told me that if I didn't help him immediately, he'd probably die. The first question I asked her was, "Is your friend a Christian?" As I previously mentioned, there is no sense in casting demons out of a non-believer, as there is nothing to keep the demons from returning.

Well, she told me her friend was not a Christian, but because of the desperation of the situation, I agreed to see him. I told her the first thing I would do is lead him to receive Jesus Christ as Lord and Savior and get him saved. She brought him to me the next day, and he looked like living death. He was heavily medicated and looked like he could pass out any moment.

As I tried to get him to receive Jesus Christ as Savior, he argued with me using what is now a very familiar argument. He said, "What kind of a God would allow an innocent little boy to be abused like I was?" His history was that he grew up in Chicago where the winters are extreme and the temperatures can drop forty degrees overnight. His mother was appallingly abusive. To punish him, she'd make him sleep in the doghouse overnight in the dead of winter, and of course, he was still bearing the scars of that abuse up until his late forties.

I explained generational sin to him and how it works. I told him about the sins of the parents being visited upon the children according to Exodus 20:5 and 34:7. I also explained that because God has given mankind a free will, He will not go against that free will. So when our parents choose evil over good, choose to serve and obey Satan rather than God, that opens a door for demons to enter into them. The demons will then cause them to perpetrate vile behavior against their children. The children suffer the consequences of those sinful choices.

I also showed him in Exodus where it shows God's loving nature: " ... showing mercy to thousands to those who love Me and keep my commandments" (Exodus 20:5, NIV). I explained to him God's extravagant love and how He visits His love to a thousand generations of those who love Him and obey Him. I also showed him in Deuteronomy where it says, "I call heaven and earth as witnesses today against you, that I have set before you life and death, blessing and cursing; therefore choose life, that both you and your descendants may live" (Deuteronomy 30:10, NIV). I told him that those verses show God pleading with His people to choose obedience so that they could be blessed. God is a good God.

He was satisfied with that and proceeded to say the sinner's prayer and received Jesus Christ as His Lord and Savior. I then went to work and first healed the wounded little boy and then began the process of casting out the demons of rejection, child abuse, rebellion, suicide, depression, death, and a multitude of others under those categories.

He was gloriously set free, went off all medication immediately, started attending church, and God gloriously restored him in every area. He was offered a better job in Colorado than the one he lost in Arizona; last I heard from him, he was thinking of attending Marilyn Hickey's Bible College in Denver. This is one true story about a man amongst multitudes who are receiving victory and freedom through the glorious ministry of deliverance. Satan wanted to destroy Al—not only in this life, but for eternity. But God had other plans for Al. Thank you, Jesus!

Open Doors for the Demonic

How do demons gain access into our lives? Here are some of the ways:

The first is sin—our own personal sin. Walking in disobedience to God's Word and ways opens the door to curses, and demons ride in on curses. Willful disobedience ultimately leads a person into bondage. "Know ye not, to whom ye yield yourselves servants to obey, his servants ye are whom you obey; whether of sin unto death, or of obedience unto righteousness" (Romans 6:16, KJV). Any act we commit, knowing the Bible forbids it, is sin. We are willfully choosing to sin.

Childhood traumas and hurts, such as abuse or rejection. This is a big open door for the demonic. Whenever the parents are not a godly covering for their children, those children are then uncovered and fair game for the demonic, and demons hate children. The best gift you can give your child is to walk closely with the Lord; it will give them the greatest covering. The greatest brunt of that responsibility lies on the father. God holds fathers in greater accountability because He has ordained for the fathers to be the spiritual heads of their households. They are to be the "priests" to their family, to teach them the ways of God. That's the order of things in God's kingdom. When the men fail to do that, they are, in essence, handing their children over to the devil.

When children are abused by their authority figures, they not only have the emotional wounding, but also demons enter in to compound that pain, and then strongholds are established around that wounding. God has provided the remedy, and it is inner healing and deliverance.

Inheritance—and this is one of the major ways that demons enter in. They are transferred genetically. In fact ninety-nine percent of what we deal with in the ministry is generational, and we automatically treat it as such. Through years of dealing with the demonic, I have discovered that if you treat the demons as generational, it brings genuine freedom to the client. If not, I have not had such good success. Also, as I take the person's family history, I see instantly that they are just repeating the patterns of their ancestors.

We break the generational curses off of yourself, your bloodline, and all future generations. We're not just concerned with you; we're concerned with your descendants. God wants them to be free from those curses as well.

If your ancestors broke God's laws and sinned against God, this opened a door for the demonic to enter into their lives. If the sin was not repented of, it then becomes a generational curse, and the demons carrying the curse now have a right to the bloodline until someone comes along and asks forgiveness for the sins and renounces the sins and breaks the curses that came in. Then it is cleared in the heavenly ledger book. Otherwise there will be that iniquitous pull toward a particular type of sin, and it will gain strength with each generation if not dealt with.

Witchcraft—and this is an umbrella for all types of occult practices. It is basically seeking contact with the spirit world through mediums, ESP, charms, tarot cards, horoscopes, incantations, astrology, pendulums, mental telepathy, yoga, oriental meditation, automatic handwriting, karate, Dungeons and Dragons, and other demonic games.

Yoga has its roots in middle eastern religions. The word yoga means "to yoke" in Sanskrit. It involves a system of physical exercise designed to control the internal organs and metabolism of the body. Yoga is a Hindu system of philosophy with at least six schools of thought. The supposed aim is to reach a state of super consciousness through eight stages of physical and mental preparation. It is claimed that miraculous powers such as levitation and invisibility may be reached when in the higher levels.

Hatha yoga involves the massage of the internal organs as an aid to relaxation and meditation. Meditation normally commences with the droning sound of incantation. Names of Hindu demonic deities and words of worship are then added. The biblical word for this exercise is idolatry. Satan loves to see Christians operating under the power of his spirit rather than the Holy Spirit.

Karate as well as all martial arts are inextricably linked to Zen Buddhism and the Buddhist philosophy. Therefore, anything that has its roots in middle eastern religions is a forbidden practice for a Christian and brings curse upon the participating Christian. God looks upon it as idolatry.

Dungeons and Dragons is a board game which is extremely dangerous for a Christian. It is essentially a feeding program for occultism and witchcraft. Many of the materials contain authentic magical rituals. The game indulges in murder, arson, torture, rape and sexual violence. In fact a man who was a witch and high priest and also involved in Satanism says that the producer of the game came to visit him. They wanted to make certain the rituals were authentic.

Vows taken by our ancestors and ourselves, such as the vows taken in the Freemason organizations—those vows are binding until they are broken and repented of.

Curses spoken against someone in our bloodline. I have ministered to two people whose lives were affected by someone putting a curse on their bloodline, and I will give you those case histories a little later so that you'll see the reality of this fact.

False religions such as Mormonism and Jehovah's Witnesses, which are clearly heretical in their attitudes to Jesus Christ, or which are specifically non- or anti-Christian in their belief system such as Buddhism, Sikhism, Islam, and Hinduism.

All of these are deceptions. Many of them are hundreds or, in some cases, thousands of years old. They were devised by Satan as a means of attracting worship to himself via the deceptions of religious demons.

Listening to satanically inspired heavy metal rock music. This opens doors for those demons of lust, fornication, debauchery, drugs, and drunkenness to enter in. I did a heavy deliverance on a gentleman in Canada who'd listened to that type of music in his youth, and twenty years later was still being tormented by the demons that entered into him. His story is in the next chapter.

Our Web site www.healing-deliverance.com is being visited by people from all around the world—Malaysia, South Africa, Canada, Nigeria, Saudi Arabia—who are desperate for deliverance. In as many cases as I can, I schedule telephone deliverances since there is no distance in the spirit realm, and the deliverances are just as successful as in-person deliverances. It is the Holy Spirit who is omnipresent who does the delivering anyway.

I ministered to an underground pastor of a Christian church in Saudi Arabia. He had found the Isaiah 61 Web site and felt like he should have deliverance as he had never had it. He was amazed at the things that came out of him as he threw up demon after demon—all things from his life before Christ and, of course, generational issues. He was so excited that he is now bringing the ministry of deliverance to his underground church, and the demand is so great that he is overwhelmed.

SATANICALLY INSPIRED HEAVY METAL MUSIC

A gentleman from Canada named Pedro called me for help. He was being tormented by demons, seeing things like bats flying around his room when there was no possible way for a bat to get into his house. As I interviewed him, I found that he had a history of failure, inability to keep jobs, poverty, and hopelessness. He also was operating under a great deal of mental confusion. He was of Portuguese descent, and his family had a strong history of witchcraft—séances, tarot cards, and all types of occult things—and I knew immediately that this was what was causing the failure in his life, the poverty.

Any brush with the occult brings a curse with it. He also told me that he had listened to a lot of demonic/satanic rock music from ages fourteen to twenty-three. He hadn't listened to it for some twenty years now, yet he was still hearing the words from some of the demonic songs in his head. It was tormenting him. This music, he said, also led him to a lot of sexual perversion, drugs, and suicide attempts.

As I ministered to him, I had him ask forgiveness for both his own involvement in the occult, satanic music, and the involvement of his ancestors—both on his mother's and father's side of the bloodline. I had him renounce those sins, and then I cast out the occult demons and the sexual perversion demons, all of which manifested very, very strongly. Then I called up the demons of satanic music, and as the demon took him over, I heard a loud roaring like the roaring of a lion. It sounded like the jungles of Africa.

Immediately following the roar, I heard a remarkably deep voice say, "He's mine. I have him. I will destroy him. *I hate him! He will be destroyed!* He will be destroyed." When I commanded the demon to renounce his claim to Pedro and all future generations, the demon shouted at me, "I shall not!" I quoted Philippians 2:9–10 to the demon, "For God has highly exalted him and given him a name that is above every name, that at the name of Jesus, every knee shall bow, of things in the heavens, on the earth and below the earth to the Glory of God." The demon started to cry and moan as though in pain, but he still wouldn't cooperate and renounce his claim to Pedro.

Then I asked him if he had a legal right to stay, and the demon said, "Yes, he belongs to me. He put himself under the pentagram, and he invoked me. I will not leave him; he is mine. I know he wants to be set free, but I will not let him." I want to stress that we do not converse with demons but simply interrogate them to get key information that is vital to the client's freedom, much like a prisoner of war might be interrogated. If we were to try and get any other information from the demonic realm, we would be entering into divination, which is forbidden in the Bible.

I then commanded the demon to go down, so I could talk to Pedro. Pedro then told me that, yes indeed, in July 1987, as he was listening to a satanic rock group called Merciful Fate and It's King Diamond, he followed the instructions of what the song was telling him to do. He went into his parents' basement and drew a pentagram and took a cross as he sang these words to the song, "You're gonna go into the coven and become Lucifer's son."

I then had Pedro specifically renounce that ritual and ask forgiveness for doing it, then called the demon back up. The demon that had been so strong, roaring like a lion, was now as meek as a lamb. He'd lost his legal right and meekly renounced his claim to Pedro and had to go when I commanded. Pedro was absolutely amazed at what had transpired. Prior to this, he only half-heartedly believed that there were actual demons in him—after all, wasn't he a Christian?

I am telling you this case history so that parents who are reading this book will become aware of what their children may actually be listening to on their iPods. There is such a danger in the wave of satanic heavy metal rock groups that have risen up in our culture. Parents, for the most part, are not even aware of what their children are listening to. Of course, there are many godly, wise parents out there who monitor what their children listen to and watch on TV and on the Internet; unfortunately, some do not. I pray that this will be a wake-up call for those parents.

We are going to be dealing with a whole generation of demonized young people who are listening to satanically inspired music and unknowingly making covenants with Satan, just as this young man had done. We had better be prepared with the knowledge of how to break these curses off of them and set them free from the demons that enter into them through that music. Prayers won't do much in situations where demons are involved. To prove that point, I can tell you that I've talked to hundreds upon hundreds of Christians who've told me they'd been prayed for by some of the most anointed people and nothing every changed. Demons don't mind having the person prayed over, as they know they can resume their demonic activity in that person as soon as the praying is done. We will have to know how to cast them out as Jesus did. Demons do not respond to anything except being commanded to leave in the name of Jesus!

As is evidenced in the case with Pedro, the interrogation process is invaluable. Deliverance ministries who've had valid experience in healing and deliverance will admit that demons can and do sometimes speak. Even the Scripture accounts validate that point. Although there is only one deliverance case in the Gospels in which Jesus entered into conversation with the demons—the Gadarene demoniac incident in Luke 8:26–29 and the parallel passage in Mark 5:1–20. What that account shows is that it was a necessary thing to do for even Jesus, the Son of God. The second thing that account shows us is the importance of knowing the name of the demon you're dealing with. We also have to remember that it tells us in John 21:25, "Jesus did many other things as well. If every one of them were written down, the whole world could not contain the books." So one account is all that is needed to be our guideline.

I teach my ministry team that we are not to seek information unrelated to the client's freedom and deliverance, or it would be like going to a medium. We are not interested in anything else the demon has to say. Isaiah 61 Ministries is run with very tight guidelines. I do not allow anything unbiblical to go on.

SPOKEN CURSES

Let's look at the reality of the sixth open door to the demonic—curses spoken against someone in our bloodline. I ministered to a young lady named Tanya, who is featured in the testimony section of our Web site. She was brought to the ministry by one of my deliverance ministers who had met her at a chiropractor's office.

We happened to be having a group deliverance when she first showed up at the ministry. As I proceeded to minister deliverance to the group, she started to manifest very heavily. As I walked over to minister to her (at that point I knew nothing about her—she was just a face in the crowd), the Holy Spirit started telling me that someone had put a curse on her bloodline.

In talking to her after the group deliverance, I found that she had a whole host of illnesses and diseases that she was being treated for at the Mayo Clinic in Phoenix, Arizona. She told me they had no cure for her illnesses, only medication. She then handed me two sheets of her medical history. I could not believe my eyes when I looked at her sheet. She had hypoglycemia, which was so extreme that she had to eat every couple of hours and get up in the middle of the night to eat. She also had Raynaud's disease, colitis, asthma, vertigo, nausea, facial pain, and extreme light/noise/motion sensitivity. She had also had a spinal fusion, spontaneous leakage in the spinal cord at the base of her brain, persistent cold sores, and the list went on.

She was a beautiful Christian young lady and obviously in desperate need of help. I immediately scheduled a personal appointment for her.

The thing that tormented her the most was extreme migraine headaches, which caused her face to droop on one side and numbness down her right arm and leg. The Mayo clinic had treated her migraines with Vioxx, Topamax, Verapamil, Keppra, Neurontin, Indomethacin, Protonix, Cymbalta, Celexa, and also tried Botox injections for the migraines—all to no avail! The migraines were so bad that she couldn't hold down a job.

When she came in for her individual deliverance, she brought her mother with her who happened to be a retired medical doctor—an internist. In taking her family history, I found that there was a lot of premature death and strange accidents, which I knew were the result of this curse that the Holy Spirit had told me about.

Her brother died when he was fourteen due to an aneurism on the brain, her aunt died six years later on the exact date when she'd gone for surgery to have a tumor removed, and Tanya herself had a spontaneous leakage at the base of her spinal cord, despite having been in no accidents or experiencing trauma to the body.

I then took her through the procedure of forgiving anyone who'd hurt her, and then had her ask forgiveness for her own personal sins (before Christ) and the known sins of her ancestors. She renounced those sins and broke their curses both on her mother's and father's side of the bloodline and off of herself, her bloodline, and all future generations.

I then proceeded with the deliverance and broke the curse that was put on the bloodline; the Holy Spirit gave me the year the curse was initiated as 1842. I called up that demon behind that spoken curse. It came up *so strong* and mocking; I found out that the curse had indeed been put on the family in Czechoslovakia in a little village called Kriska. The demon started to speak in Czechoslovakian, which Tanya herself did not know in the natural.

It was a very strong deliverance; after it was cast out, her mother said that she remembered her grandmother telling her that someone had indeed put a curse on the family back in Czechoslovakia. I then went for all the different illnesses that were brought on by this curse and cast them out one by one. She was immediately healed of every single sickness and disease for which even the Mayo Clinic had no answer.

In fact, prior to the deliverance, the neurologist at the Mayo Clinic whom she'd been seeing for the last two years was recommending that he put in an occipital nerve stimulator (a computer chip implanted in her head with a battery pack implanted in her abdomen and a remote control). As a result of that deliverance session, she was healed of Reynaud's disease, which caused numbness and cold in her hands and feet, hypoglycemia, vertigo, migraines, yeast infections, herpes virus (cold sores) in her mouth, colitis, irritable bowel syndrome, and a host of other things like terrifying nightmares. She is one very thankful young lady and a walking, talking miracle. She told me afterwards that it challenged a lifetime of work for her mother. Thank you, Jesus, the Great Physician!

INVOLVEMENT IN WITCHCRAFT AND ITS CONSEQUENCES

Let's look at the fourth door that gives demons access into our lives—witchcraft. If there's been any brush with the occult in your bloodline and in your personal life, it has opened the door for curse upon you and your descendants. Some of the evidence of a family or individual being under an occultic curse is the occurrence of strange accidents, premature death, automobile accidents, mental confusion, and poverty.

God's Word absolutely condemns and forbids all witchcraft practices. Deuteronomy 13:10–12 says, "Let no one be found among you who sacrifices his son or daughter in the fire, who practices divination or sorcery, interprets omens, engages in witchcraft, or casts spells, or who is a medium or spiritist or who consults the dead. Anyone who does these things is detestable to the Lord."

Notice the words "casts spells." Isn't that what all the Harry Potter books and movies are teaching our young children? It is not innocent stuff. It brings a curse with it. What might appear at a surface level to be harmless or innocent has great significance in the unseen spirit world. I remember one of my ministry people telling me that they had watched a game show sometime back and the question was asked, "What has been found to cause seizures in children?" The answer was "Pokemon." They said that research was done on the unusual amount of children going to doctors with seizures. What they found was that the seizures started when they started watching Pokemon on television and got Pokemon toys and games in their possession. The Pokemon characters were named after Japanese demons.

Witchcraft and sorcery in the bloodline will almost always lead to drug abuse in future generations. I have discovered in ministering to those who've been in bondage to drugs that there was almost always sorcery or witchcraft in the bloodline which opened the door to drug addiction in their lives. Poverty is another spirit that operates over anyone who's been into the occult or who has had a heavy bloodline history of the same. I have seen this personally in ministering to people. We also have a classic example of this in countries like Haiti or India, where there's witchcraft and voodoo on every corner. These are some of the most impoverished nations in the world.

Let me show you the reality of what dabbling in witchcraft can bring upon your family and your descendants.

Real Life Deliverances

I ministered to a man many years ago who was in a worship band in the church I attended at that time. His wife had come to me and told me that although her husband was a born again, spirit-filled believer he still struggled with some things. She felt he needed deliverance.

I arranged for a private deliverance session for him. When I interviewed him, I found that he'd gotten saved when he was in jail on drug abuse charges. His family history was one of total destruction and dysfunction.

He had grown up in a typical "druggie family" with both parents on drugs; of course, he followed in their footsteps. Stepping into that same arena, he started his self-destructive life style at age fourteen. He had also run away from home several times at age fourteen due to all the neglect and abuse in his home.

He proceeded to tell me that his father had seven brothers, who were all the town thugs—bootleggers first and then drug dealers. They lived in California at the time, and the police kept a watch on all of them at all times because of their terrible reputation.

Well, when this man, whom we'll call John for the sake of anonymity, was in jail, his father came to visit him. His father had come to the Lord Jesus Christ through a wonderful nationwide program called Teen Challenge. He then prayed with his son to receive Jesus Christ as Lord and Savior. Then when John left prison, he enrolled in Teen Challenge and learned the things of God, and his life was turned around. However, he was still struggling because those curses and demons had not been cast out.

As we proceeded with the session I had John ask forgiveness for witchcraft and sorcery, as I know from experience that if it's somewhere in the bloodline, it will lead to drug addiction or alcoholism.

Then after taking him through all the formalities, such as forgiving others who'd hurt him, asking forgiveness for his own personal sins and the sins of his ancestors, I proceeded with the deliverance.

The first thing I called up was witchcraft, and I wasn't prepared for how strong the spirit was, as he was a very mild-mannered man. It quickly blurted out John's family history, which I discovered at the close of the session he was unaware of. Again, let me put in a disclaimer here as I always do. I do not, nor do I allow my ministry team, to converse with demons. However, we do allow for any information that is a key to that person's freedom. Demons or unclean spirits are of the spirit world, and they hold onto that information as though it were yesterday. There is no time element in the spirit world. To the spirit world what happened in 1600 is just as vividly recalled as what happened last week.

I pointed out before the biblical precedent in Luke 8:26–39 and Mark 5:1–20 where even Jesus, who was the Son of God, had to have quite an extended conversation with the demons in the Gadarene demoniac. If it was the necessary thing for Jesus to do, wouldn't it also hold true for us? Once again, this case, like hundred of others, shows us the necessity of getting the name of the demons you're dealing with. Now there may be some reading this book who are thinking we should simply allow the Holy Spirit to give us the names of the demons and the deeper issues involved. Unfortunately, the Holy Spirit usually doesn't show us through words of knowledge alone all the information deliverance ministers need to set the person totally free. He has provided an additional tool by forcing, under His anointing, the demons to give us the rest of the information needed for the person's freedom. When the demons aren't strong enough to speak, I have done entire deliverances by allowing the Holy Spirit to give me the names of the demons.

Not every deliverance minister is that tuned in to the Holy Spirit. If I'm tired, I don't hear as clearly as I'd like to, and that's why God has provided another way. I'm sure that's the reason He allowed the above scriptures to be in the Bible as our instruction.

That spirit of witchcraft blurted out that John's family was a very prominent family in Wales, very close to the Queen of Wales, and also very close to God. God had a hedge of protection around the family. That is until a man named Simon in the family got into witchcraft; by the seventeenth century, the family that was once esteemed by the Queen of Wales and protected by God, was driven out of Wales because of the witchcraft and eventually came to America. It was the degeneration of a fine family line. As soon as the witchcraft entered into the bloodline, the hedge God had put around the family was removed. The once prominent family that had been blessed by God became a bloodline of thugs and criminals. In talking to the man after the deliverance, he said it made sense, as he'd always been attracted to Welsh-type music but never knew his ethnic background.

Although the above case history relates to witchcraft, it can be other sins that cause God's protection to be removed from our family and us. If we look at the book of Job, we will see the biblical principle of protection laid out very clearly.

> One day the angels came to present themselves before the Lord, and Satan also came with them. The Lord said to Satan, "Where have you come from?" Satan answered the Lord, "From roaming through the earth and going back and forth in it." Then the Lord said to Satan, "Have you considered my servant Job? There is no one on earth like him; he is blameless and upright, a man who fears God and shuns evil." "Does Job fear God for nothing?" Satan replied. "Have you not put a *hedge* around him and his household and everything he has? You have blessed the work of his hands, so that his flocks and herds are spread throughout the land. But stretch out your hand and strike everything he has, and he will surely curse you to your face."
>
> Job 1:6–11 (NIV)

The book of Job shows that God was testing Job, and it was not because he had stepped into sin. We see that because Job feared (revered) God in his life and walked in total obedience to God; a hedge was put around him, his loved ones, and his possessions. This is still true today because God is the same yesterday, today, and forever. His principles and laws are eternal.

For those who still don't believe that Christians can have demons, let me give you the case of a woman named Maureen who just recently moved from Florida to Arizona to be a part of the Isaiah 61 deliverance ministry. She was an intelligent, educated woman who was an education consultant for the school districts. She also grew up in a pastor's home and had been a Christian for as long as she could remember.

However, about a month after she joined my ministry team, she called me to say that she thought some witchcraft had transferred to her. She'd come home from work feeling really sick. She thought she'd have to be rushed to the hospital, as she was feeling faint, nauseous, running hot and cold, and feeling very, very weak. I started to cast witchcraft out of her over the phone, and that spirit was screaming in the most incredible high-pitched sound I'd ever heard. There's nothing as hideous as a witchcraft spirit being cast out. The sound is high-pitched and extremely eerie.

Well, some of it went, but not all of it. I then questioned her and found that despite the fact that her father was a pastor, she'd been involved with Ouija boards, levitation, and horoscopes as a young girl at slumber parties. As an adult, she had also traveled a great deal and walked on some very unholy ground, resulting in curses coming upon her. She'd been to Egyptian tombs, and Pagan temples, etc. These pagan places have demons guarding them, and some demons may transfer to the people coming through.

After taking her through renunciations, I cast out the unclean spirits of all of those occult things, and she had a very strong deliverance. She's a very godly, Christ-like, mild-mannered woman, but she had one of the strongest deliverances I'd seen in a long time. All of those spirits came out screaming and wailing.

In discussing the deliverance with her later, she told me that she was surprised that all of those things were in her, as she had gone through different "deliverances" (at least what was labeled deliverance, yet proved to be ineffective at best) in some of the churches she'd been a part of in Florida. She told me she'd never manifested like that before. She just took what they said by faith. They told her that she was delivered, and she had believed it.

I also did a deliverance on a young woman who had recurring accidents, always the same time of the year. In questioning her, I found that before she became a Christian, she'd read horoscopes faithfully and thought she was a Libra. Well, her birthday was October fifteenth, and the recurring automobile accidents took place around that time each year. She was under the curse of Libra. So I took her through renunciation and had her declare that she was not a Libra but rather a child of God, washed in the blood of Jesus. The curse of Libra had no authority over her, and she was set free.

Another thing I have found in ministering to individuals is that sometimes witchcraft in the bloodline is tied to sicknesses like lupus, fibromyalgia, and lymphatic cancer.

One example is a woman whom I ministered to many years ago who was born in Puerto Rico, which has a heavy history of witchcraft. After I broke the generational curse of witchcraft off of her, she was instantly healed of lupus, fibromyalgia, and tumors that were in her stomach and had caused her stomach to be distended.

A lovely Christian lady whom I ministered to had been born in London. She came for deliverance for an advanced case of lymphoma. In interviewing her, I found that growing up in London there was witchcraft on every corner. Her grandmother was in a witches' coven, was a high priestess, and had exposed this dear lady from the age of three to eight years of age to the rituals in the coven. After we broke the curse of that witchcraft and had her renounce any satanic dedications that were made over her, I cast the cancer out of her body; the lymph node, which was severely swollen under her chin, was healed—no more swelling. The lymph node on the side of her neck, which had been the size of a small lemon, was also healed.

An almost unbelievable story came from a woman whom I'll call Val. It seems that when she was a little girl, her mother was completely immersed in the occult. This mother called up the spirit of Val's dead grandmother during a séance she held. From that point on, the things that happened were absolutely bizarre. We in the Christian world are so completely ignorant of what those who dabble in darkness are capable of.

She went on to say that shortly after her mother had done this, the phone rang, and Val went to answer it only to hear the voice of her dead grandmother on the line. She dropped the phone in terror and went screaming for her mother. It gets worse. A few days after that, she heard a car pull up to the front of her house. As she looked out the front window, she saw her dead grandmother get out of the cab and walk toward the front door. She had on the same clothes she'd been buried in.

The little girl went screaming in terror for her mother. When the mother saw this dead grandmother at the front door, she went into a panic and right there dropped to her knees and repented of her witchcraft. We need to be aware of some of this stuff the occult has unleashed upon our nation like never before, and we need to know how to battle it.

A Pastor's wife from Oregon came to one of my services recently. A friend of hers from Oregon had found our Web site and had flown into Phoenix to come to the ministry. Her friend had taken pictures of me from the back of the room as I was teaching, and the Pastor's wife said when her friend had the pictures developed, it showed huge angels with swords drawn covering the complete back wall, waiting for me to start the group deliverance so that they could assist in the battle.

When I called her after she got back to Oregon to ask for a copy of the picture, she started to tell me her dark childhood history. Apparently her dad was a high satanic priest, and she said she saw huge demons in her home all the time and was in constant terror. Then one day she saw a woman in a store who had a bright, luminous aura all around her. She went to her and asked her why she had all that light around her. The woman told her it was the light of Jesus Christ that surrounds all believers and told her about Jesus for the first time and invited her to church. Julie got saved.

The interesting thing she told me was that those in the occult—Satanism and witchcraft—can see in the spirit realm, and once your eyes are open to the spirit realm, you always see. She said she can still see darkness around people who don't have Christ in their lives and an aura of light around those who are Christians. She can also see demons and angels.

She shared the struggle that ensued in her body and soul after salvation, and how she went from church to church and pastor to pastor seeking help, knowing she needed deliverance, but everyone thought she was crazy. All because the enemy has convinced the church that either demons don't exist, or if they do, they can't possibly be in Christians. When she became a Christian is when the battle began. Prior to that, she belonged to the kingdom of darkness. Once she got saved, she had switched allegiance to the kingdom of light, and the demons that were in her started to manifest powerfully. She told me how very much a true deliverance ministry like mine is needed.

There were also at least three known cases of women who had gone through my group deliverance on witchcraft and the occult who were immediately healed of allergies to cats. I don't know the exact correlation between witchcraft and cat allergies, but I do know that they were completely healed. It's probably that cats were used in some sort of witchcraft ritual somewhere in their ancestry. None of these ladies were aware of any witchcraft in their bloodline, which is why it pays to go through all the group deliverances I hold. We never know what's at the root of a certain illness.

I was doing a group deliverance on witchcraft and the occult, and a young mother came for the first time with her eleven-year-old son. They sat way in the back, having been invited by someone and not quite sure of what they were getting into. Well, when I broke the curse of witchcraft in people's bloodline and commanded the spirits of witchcraft out, I saw her young son turn red and start coughing; his body started to contort, as a demon was obviously manifesting in him.

I went over to minister to him, but it wouldn't leave. Then the Holy Spirit spoke to me and said, "It's Harry Potter." So I asked the mother if he was into Harry Potter, and she looked surprised and said, "Yes, but I didn't think there was anything wrong with it." I explained to her that it's all about witchcraft and teaching kids how to cast spells, and it brings the child under a curse of the occult, which God forbids us to dabble in. He renounced it, and I was then able to cast out the spirit that was tormenting him, quickly and without any more resistance.

As I was ministering to an eighteen-year-old just recently, he told me a chilling story about what his dad experienced when he was in college. He said that in his dad's dorm there was a young man who was very heavily into the board game Dungeons and Dragons. One night, a demon obviously took this young man over because he came screaming into his dad's dorm room brandishing a sword and threatening to kill every-one in the room. It took five big football players to wrestle the sword from him and try to pin him down. As they were trying to pin him down, this demonized young man was actually levitating. Needless to say, Dungeons and Dragons is a very, very dangerous game. What people do is call up demons when they dabble with the occult; once the demon takes a person over, there's no telling what they will cause that person to do.

Some of the nationalities that have a heavy preponderance of witchcraft in their bloodline are Mexican people, Puerto Rican people, and many others from South American countries. I've ministered to many of Mexican descent, and they told me that all their relatives go to witch doctors to receive "healings" or to put curses on their enemies. Many go to the witch doctors to have them cast a spell on someone they want to marry. Also in Mexico, the Mayans still go to "the high places" spoken of in the Old Testament to offer baby sacrifices.

I remember a Christian missionary in Mexico telling the story of how he was invited by some Mayans to go to the top of a mountain when there was a full moon to see the ritual that was performed by these Mayans. So out of curiosity, he went. He told of the terrifying experience as they sat around a circle, and some were beating on drums, while others built an altar and then kindling for a fire under it. He said all of a sudden, he felt such an ominous and oppressive darkness come over the place.

Before he knew what was happening, they'd placed a newborn baby on the altar and were about to light the fire. At that exact moment, a wolf started to howl and came slinking out of the darkness toward the group. He said he reacted in a heartbeat and snatched the baby off the altar! As soon as he did that, the wolf turned around and ran down the side of the mountain, and the fearful darkness that permeated the atmosphere lifted. As shaken as he was, he was able to tell these Mayans about Jesus and what they were about to do was from Satan. He then led these people to the Lord, but the experience is one he has never been able to shake off.

CATHOLICISM

Having been raised a Catholic, I have personal experience on the teachings of the Catholic Church. I didn't come into salvation until the age of thirty-eight, at which time the eyes of my understanding were opened as I began to read the Bible for the first time in my life.

One evening as I was holding a group deliverance for those who came out of Catholicism, and some very interesting things transpired. Now if you're not familiar with the history of Catholicism, you need to do some reading on the subject. Catholicism is heavily into idolatry and pagan practices, which they incorporate into their daily masses. The worship and prayer to saints (who are nothing more than deceased human beings, and we are not to pray to human beings; this is basic idolatry) and to the "Blessed Virgin Mary" are all an abomination to God. The Bible calls this idolatry and makes it clear we are to pray only to the Father, through His Son, Jesus Christ.

The rosary beads were taken from pagan religions. The use of these beads started in 1090 AD and were copied from the Hindus and the Mohammedans.

Mary is elevated above Jesus in many instances, and Catholics are instructed to pray to Mary, to get to her son

Jesus, with the belief being, "After all, who knows the heart of Jesus better than his mother?" However, God's Word tells us clearly, "There is one mediator between God and man, the Lord Jesus Christ" (1 Timothy 2:5).

Mary is made to be very powerful, and Jesus in many cases is relegated to a weak little infant baby that she carries in her arms. Nowhere in the Bible does it tell us to pray to Mary, or to the "saints." Some good reference materials on *Catholicism are Examination of The Council of Trent* by Martin Chemnitz. It is a synopsis on the Council of Trent from a Protestant viewpoint. Others are *A History of the Council of Trent* by Jedin, and *New Catholic Encyclopedia, supplements* 1978–1988, *Volume* 18. In these texts, you will find the historical facts that I list in this chapter and the dates that they were introduced into Catholicism, while the Catholic Church claims that it never changes. I will also tell you what the Bible says about some of these things.

The worship of Mary and the use of the term Mother of God started in 431 AD. God's Word tells us we are to have no other Gods before Him. In Matthew the twelfth chapter, it says, "While Jesus was still talking to the crowd, his mother and brothers, stood outside wanting to speak to him. Someone told him, 'Your mother and brothers are standing outside, wanting to speak to you.' He replied to him, 'Who is my mother, and who are my brothers?' Pointing to his disciples, he said, 'Here are my mother and my brothers. For whoever does the will of my Father in heaven is my brother and sister and mother.'"

What we see here is that if Mary was to be worshipped, Jesus would have taken this opportunity to show us that. Yet what he did was quite the opposite response. He purposefully brought her down to a very human level stating that everyone who does the will of His Father is His family. I believe that God looked down the corridor of time and knowing man's propensity to exalt Mary to a higher level than an obedient human being, used this scriptural example to dispel that error. Mary is not deity; she was an obedient young woman who properly responded to a calling. The above scripture account shows that she was a sinner in need of a Savior, just like you and I.

Mary is also called Queen of Heaven in the Catholic Church, and that term comes from Jeremiah: "… the women make cakes of bread for the Queen of Heaven" (Jeremiah 7:18, NIV). In this verse, God was talking about the abominations that His people were engaged in—the worship of other gods. Most of the heathen nations in the Old Testament worshipped female goddesses.

The immaculate conception of the Virgin Mary was proclaimed in 1854. This means that Mary was conceived without a human father by the Holy Spirit, just as Jesus was. This heresy of elevating Mary above Jesus Christ developed during the middle ages.

Transubstantiation came in 1215 AD. This teaches the false heresy that the bread and wine in the Mass are magically changed into the literal flesh and literal blood of Jesus. This is nothing but black witchcraft. The Bible teaches us to take the bread and cup, which is *symbolic* of the body and blood of Christ, not the literal body and blood.

Confession of sins to a priest at least once a year was commanded in 1215 AD. The adoration and worship of the host (the bread), which has the Egyptian symbol of the goddess Isis stamped on it, was decreed in 1220 AD. This is all idolatry, which is the basic sin of the Catholic Church.

They forbade the Bible to laymen in 1229 AD and took the Scriptures away from the people. In 1439 AD, the doctrine of the seven sacraments was affirmed. There are no sacraments. For example, baptism and the Lord's Supper are for believers. In 1870 AD, the pope suddenly decided that he was infallible—this means when he speaks he is literally speaking the word of God.

This is an abomination. It tells us in John 1 that Jesus is the Living Word—not any human being.

Yet any one of us who came out of Catholicism can tell you that the Catholic Church teaches and proclaims that it never changes.

As I stated earlier, I was raised a Catholic and didn't get saved until I was thirty-eight years of age, so I know the reality of what I've just outlined for you. Catholics are good people who need to read the Word of God for themselves to find truth! Jesus said, "You shall know the truth and the truth shall make you free" (John 8:32, NIV). It was a defining moment for me when the priests in my parish told me not to question the Church's teachings and that it was unnecessary to read the Bible. My daughter still remembers a third grade religion class at her Catholic elementary school, where the priests told her the story of Jonah and the whale could not have possibly happened. That it is just symbolic and metaphorical!

While it is not my intent to hurt anyone, I must stress that it is only in reading the Bible that we come into the knowledge of God; everything else is simply religious tradition that nullifies the Word of God. That's why Jesus died for us at the cross of Calvary so that the veil between mankind and God would forever be removed. So we could know God for ourselves, and seek God for ourselves. We no longer need a priest to be our mediator. That's what the Protestant Reformation was all about. Thank God for men like Martin Luther, who suffered immense persecution in order to make the Bible available to every man and woman.

Jesus Christ is our Great High Priest and the only mediator between God and man. The priesthood has been done away with once and for all. That was the Old Testament system. Only the priests could come into the Holy of Holies and approach God on behalf of mankind. Now, hallelujah, each and every one of us has that ability. We can enter into the Holy of Holies, covered in the blood of the Lamb; when we do, the Father receives us because we come in the righteousness of Jesus, not our own righteousness. Jesus has made us one of His own. When we approach the throne, Jesus is right there at the right hand of the Father, saying, "Father, Eleanor has a request, and she is here in My name. She's not come in her own righteousness but in mine." The Father then says, "Yes, daughter, come boldly to my throne of grace, and tell me what's on your heart."

I recently read an article about a French Catholic nun who suffered from Parkinson's disease. Well, one night when her disease was quite unbearable, her mother superior told her to write down Pope John Paul's name on a piece of paper.

The article went on to say that the writing was practically illegible because her hand shook so much from the Parkinson's. She then prayed to the late pontiff to heal her. She went to sleep and awoke at 4:30 a.m. and bounded out of bed, having been completely healed.

It sounds good, doesn't it? My dear reader, that is what is called a "counterfeit miracle." Pope Paul is dead and cannot heal a single soul. God's Word says "…it is appointed unto man to die *once* and after this comes judgment" (Hebrews 9:27, NAS). Also in 2 Corinthians, it says: "—to be absent from the body, and to be present with the Lord" (2 Corinthians 5:8, KJV). When a person dies, he goes immediately into the presence of the Lord in heaven if he is a born again believer, having given his life to Jesus Christ when he was on the earth. If he rejected Christ, he goes immediately into the bowels of hell. The Word of God is very clear on that. We don't get a second chance, no matter what another religion may be preaching. God's Word is forever settled in heaven, and it doesn't change. To be praying to a dead man is to be praying to demons—it's called divination or necromancy, consulting the dead.

There is no man or woman, living or dead, who can do miracles and heal people. It is only the spirit of the living God moving through us who can do a miracle and heal someone. God will only use those people who are committed to Him and living their lives for Him. We human beings are only vessels that God uses to pour His power through. It is indeed a privilege and an honor to be used of God in this way, as we humbly submit ourselves to Him and give Him all the Glory! Of ourselves, we can do nothing. We couldn't heal a flea!

Satan is a counterfeiter, and he can do counterfeit miracles with the ultimate goal to lead you down a path of deception—rejecting Jesus Christ—and praying to a dead human being rather than God in order to forever damn your soul to hell. This is what the Bible calls idolatry, going to and worshipping other gods (demon gods).

Catholic Curses

To show you how powerful the curses are, I want to share with you what happened recently when I held a group deliverance on curses from Catholicism. A gentleman came in for the first time, and as I called up and broke the curse of Catholic confirmation, a huge and very powerful demon manifested in him and started to growl and distort his hands and body.

I went over to try and get him set free, but the demon wouldn't obey and leave when I commanded it to release this man. Instead it kept on growling and tormenting him. I asked why it wasn't leaving; did it have a legal right to stay? The demon said, "We've got his daughter, Christina." I said, "What do you mean you've got his daughter?" The demon responded, "We've given her throat cancer" and then started to laugh this diabolical laugh. At that point, I had the demon renounce his claim to his daughter, and then I cast it out of him. It went with great noise and throwing up. He was in shock and started weeping. He then told me his grown daughter had had throat cancer seven times and had been through seven operations for the removal of those cancers.

We were all amazed as various ones in the room remembered that the confirmation involved the Catholic bishop putting two long candles on each side of the neck and crossing the candles at the throat as the ceremony of confirmation took place. Wax candles were introduced into church ceremonies and rituals in 320 AD. Roman Catholic authorities freely admit that the use of candles in their services was lifted directly from paganism. It's witchcraft, folks, and it brings a curse as was evidenced in this man's life and family.

Once that curse was broken, guess what? He came back the next week and testified before the congregation that his daughter, who recently had yet another tumor appear in her throat, went back to the doctor for a checkup, and the tumor was completely gone. She was totally healed.

The Lord had so arranged for this man and his family to be set free. The first session he came to was the group deliverance on Catholicism, and that was a very heavy stronghold in his life. He came to the Ministry at the invitation of a friend, but not really believing in deliverance. He had been a born again believer for twenty-three years and also an elder at an established Christian church. Needless to say, he was amazed at what transpired. He was completely ignorant on the subject of curses, as much of the Christian church is. He just believed that once you become a Christian, all of the old stuff goes away.

Even as I was sitting at the computer working on this book, I received a call from this same man who is now on my Board of Directors. He had been struggling for over a year trying to find a job and had sent out hundreds of résumés to no avail. He is a very educated man and had formerly been the CEO of some large and well-known companies. There was no reason for him to have this type of failure in the natural, as he was very well qualified.

I had been praying with him for the right job to come in. I finally told him there must be some type of curse in operation, holding back that job and blessing. So we agreed in prayer that God would show him what it was so that we could break it. Well, the Lord showed him in a very vivid dream that it was the curse of praying to Mary and praying the rosary beads that were blocking his receiving the job he desired.

When I ministered to him, I had him renounce and ask forgiveness for the sin of praying to Mary and praying the rosary (which is a pagan practice) and broke the curse off of him and commanded the demon behind it to leave him. What resulted was mind-boggling. The demon didn't want to leave and was weeping and wailing and saying, "No, I can't go." I asked why it couldn't go, and it said, "I'm protecting him from jobs." Well, it's obvious the demon wasn't protecting him but cursing him from receiving the desired job. So I commanded it to leave this man and blessed him with the right job. After the curse was broken, the situation was totally reversed, and inexplicably, the job interviews began to come in.

If you need more facts on Catholicism, there are some excellent books put out by Southwest Radio Bible School that you can peruse. A book I highly recommend is *Queen of All* by Tetlow, Oakland, and Myers, exposing what's behind the Marian apparitions. Millions of gullible people are worshipping "Mary, Queen of Heaven" all over the world instead of worshipping Jesus Christ, the only begotten Son of God. He's the one who died on the cross for our sins, not Mary. He's the only way to the Father—the only way to heaven. There is *no other way*.

FREEMASONRY

Let's take a deeper look at the subject of vows taken by our ancestors or us, such as in a Freemasonry organization. If you don't know anything about Freemasonry, you need to get some Christian books exposing Freemasonry. I do an entire group deliverance on Freemasonry, and people who had no clue that Freemasonry was in their bloodline have been healed of all sorts of things.

I'm going to give you a very encapsulated look at the origins of Freemasonry:

Masonry had very innocent beginnings. It was just a building trade guild begun around the twelfth century. It was infiltrated in the seventeenth century by the Illuminati, the Rosecrusians, the agnostics, and the political elite. The organization was perverted to an occult Trojan horse within the church. In 1800, the Masonic constitution was vacuumed of every Christian influence.

Joseph Smith, the founder of the Church of Jesus Christ of the Latter Day Saints or Mormonism, was a Freemason. He taught the Masonic ritual as divine inspiration to his own leaders. The founders of Jehovah's Witnesses, Christian Science, Theosophical Society, and many other cults were all Freemasons. The founders of Freemasonry have been quoted as saying that it is far more important that men strive to become christs, (meaning they become christ themselves and do not need Jesus Christ) than that they should believe that Jesus was the Christ. The belief of modern Masonry is that man is the builder of his own immortal soul, and as such is his own savior. If he does not save himself, he will not be saved.

All of their symbols are of an astrological source: eye of Horus is a pagan deity from Egypt. They incorporate all the signs of the Zodiac. Diana (who was the goddess of Ephesus, goddess behind Mary Queen of Heaven mentioned in Jeremiah, and who Catholics worship) and Lucifer are shown as the pagan moon and stars. The certificates they give are dated AL—the year of Lucifer.

Freemasonry claims that Jesus and Lucifer are two sides of the same deity. Mormonism teaches they are both sons of God and therefore brothers. Spiritual blindness comes to ancestors of Freemasons, and their children and grandchildren are oftentimes led into strange religions, due to this inherited influence—the blindness that is invited in with the ritual of the hoodwink or blindfold.

Some churches or ministries have taken people through Freemasonry renunciations, and that's good, but unfortunately, renunciation is only the first step. Behind every renunciation, there are demons that have to be cast out. The Holy Spirit spoke to me one evening as I was in prayer and told me that I was only getting half the job done by just leading people through the renunciations, that I must now cast out the demons behind those renunciations. I was obedient, and the next session I did just that. There were *fireworks* in the room. One young woman started shaking and screaming through the entire session.

She later told me she had just come back from Colorado Springs where they had gone through the renunciations in a very large ministry, but nothing obvious had happened until now. She was a very attractive person who had extremely poor eyesight and was forced to wear thick, coke-bottle glasses. She told me she'd once been cited for driving without her glasses.

Well, about a week after the deliverance, she noticed that her glasses were bothering her, so she went to her eye doctor for what she thought would be a new prescription. He told her, "You don't need new glasses; it looks like someone did laser surgery on your eyes. You have twenty-twenty vision." This was after she renounced the oaths taken in the Shriner's portion of the Freemasonry organization that went like this: "I renounce the oaths taken and the curses and penalties involved in the Ancient Arabic Order of the Nobles of the Mystic Shrine. I renounce the piercing of the eyeballs with a three-edged blade, the flaying of the feet, the madness, and the worship of the false god Allah as the god of our fathers. I renounce the hoodwink, the mock hanging, the mock beheading, the mock drinking of the blood of the victim, the mock dog urinating on the initiate, and the offering of urine as a commemoration."

Another young mother went through the Freemasonry group deliverance, and when she got home, found that her little girl, who'd been born with a breathing disorder and had to be on a respirator, was completely healed. That healing was the result of her renouncing the first degree of Freemasonry, which causes, asthma, hay fever, and emphysema. Also in this degree we renounce the noose around the neck, which I believe causes babies to be born with the cord tied around their necks. In the third degree, there is an oath we renounce having to do with blows to the head. Thus far, I have ministered to many people who've had strange accidents, always involving blows to the head. It's hard to believe that grown men can actually take such blood-curdling oaths and think nothing of it. They are cursing their future generations.

A woman by the name of Lori, who lives in Michigan, got a hold of my Freemasonry group deliverance CDs and went through the deliverance by listening to the CDs. She called to tell me that she started manifesting very strongly as soon as she started the renunciations, and she had some miraculous physical healings as a result of the deliverance by CD.

Some of the healings she experienced was that she was able to completely stop taking her thyroid medicine—her thyroid problem was gone, hormonal imbalance was gone, and the facial hair she'd been tormented by was also completely gone. She said the greatest benefit of the deliverance was the fact that the clarity of the Bible became incredible after deliverance.

As I did some telephone deliverance on her after that, she was completely healed of bladder problems. She'd been scheduled for bladder surgery as her bladder was falling out. She told me, as I was doing deliverance on her, that she could feel the unclean spirits leaving her bladder.

Another precious saint of God, who'd just recently started attending my deliverance meetings, got up and testified that after going through the Freemasonry group deliverance, her eyesight had been restored. She was probably in her late sixties and had been a Christian for many years. However, she'd never gone through deliverance, nor was she aware that there was Freemasonry in her bloodline. She said when she would try to read at night, it was as if a film came over her eyes, and she couldn't see. She thought perhaps it was drooping eyelids and that surgery would correct it. Guess what? Dr. Jesus corrected it through the wonderful ministry of deliverance.

I'm going to give you another sampling of what types of oaths are taken in the Freemasonry organization. In the thirty-third degree we renounce "the oaths taken and the curses involved in the thirty-third degree of Masonry. I renounce and forsake the declaration that Lucifer is God. I renounce the cable-tow around the neck. I renounce the death wish that the wine drunk from a human skull should turn to poison and the skeleton whose cold arms are invited if the oath of this degree is violated." These oaths are binding until someone takes accountability and breaks them over the bloodline.

At the end of this book, you will find the Freemasonry oaths and renunciations.

SEXUAL SINS

Let's look at our own personal sins. One of the most common sins that Satan ensnares people with are sexual sins because he knows that the sexual urge in human beings is very strong. Thus it is his primary target. There are many in the body of Christ who think nothing of "sleeping around," yet God calls it a sin of fornication. It has devastating consequences.

In Jude 1:4, it says "They are godless men, who change the grace of our God into a license for immorality." Jude was referring to many first-century false teachers who were teaching that Christians could do whatever they liked without fear of God's punishment. They had a light view of God's holiness and his justice. Paul the Apostle refuted the same kind of false teaching in Romans 6:1–23. Even today in modern Christianity, some Christians minimize the seriousness of sin, believing that how they live has little to do with their faith. Too late they discover that sin has consequences.

Many Christians pick and choose which Scriptures they will obey and which they will disregard, to their own detriment. There are many scriptures in the New Testament forbidding sexual sin and they are there for our own protection. I've pulled out just a few of the scriptures–all are the NIV translation:

Galatians 5:19: "The acts of the sinful nature are obvious; sexual immorality, impurity and debauchery; idolatry and witchcraft; hatred, discord, jealousy, fits of rage, selfish ambition, dissensions, factions and envy; drunkenness, orgies, and the like. I warn you, as I did before, that those who live like this will not inherit the kingdom of God."

I Peter 4:3 "For you have spent enough time in the past doing what pagans choose to do–living in debauchery, lust, drunkenness, orgies, carousing and detestable idolatry."

James 1:21 "Therefore, get rid of all moral filth and the evil that is so prevalent and humbly accept the word planted in you, which can save you."

Hebrews 13:4 "Marriage should be honored by all, and the marriage bed kept pure, for God will judge the adulterer and all the sexually immoral."

I Thessalonians 4:5 "It is God's will that you should be sanctified; that you should avoid sexual immorality; that each of you should learn to control his own body in a way that is holy and honorable, not in passionate lust like the heathen, who do not know God—"

Colossians 3:5–7 "Put to death, therefore, whatever belongs to your earthly nature: sexual immorality, impurity, lust, evil desires and greed, which is idolatry. Because of these, the wrath of God is coming. You used to walk in these ways, in the life you once lived."

These Scriptures are not suggestions; they are commands put there by the Creator of the Universe for our safety and protection. When we walk out from under the safety and protection of God's commands which are part of Kingdom living, we enter into Satan's kingdom and Satan is a hard taskmaster. Romans 6:16 says "Know ye not, that to whom ye yield yourselves servants to obey, his servants ye are to whom ye obey; whether of sin unto death, or of obedience unto righteousness." We are all servants of the one whom we serve, either God or Satan and Satan's only plan for your life is death and destruction.

Before I proceed with the subject of sexual sin, let me tell you how the devil operates so you can recognize his tactics either in your life or in the life of your children.

The devil doesn't just come in there and announce that he's going to set up shop in your life, i.e. that he's taking you over. He's much too clever for that. He does it bit by bit. He'll seduce you into sin with the thoughts he puts in your mind and the temptations he sets before you. He'll put thoughts in your mind such as, "Well, everybody's doing it, so why shouldn't I?" Or "Well, one time isn't going to do anything. I can always walk away from it."

He may seduce you with sexual sin at first, then to salve your guilty conscience, you'll start drinking, and that will open more doors for demons to be poured into you. Before you know it, you've totally lost your moral compass and brought destruction and dishonor not only to yourself but to your children! Satan's bait is always tasty, but under that tasty morsel is a huge hook. By the time you recognize what you've swallowed, it's usually too late. Satan now has a hook in your jaw!

Soul Ties

When we become sexually intimate with someone outside the sanctity of marriage, we become one flesh with them, and their demons or curses can and do transfer to us. Soul ties are one of the ways that demons transfer back and forth, and we establish soul ties with someone that we're in sexual union with. Another thing that happens is that a part of your soul goes with them, and you receive a part of their soul. So when a person has had sex with partners, outside of the sanctity of marriage, it's as if their soul is spread out all over the place. Therefore, people who've had many sex partners are so splintered that sometimes they don't even know who they are any more. They become filled with confusion and instability and loaded with demons as well.

Let me clarify what I am saying by giving you an understanding of what comprises our soul. Man is a tri-part being, comprised of body, soul and spirit, according to 1 Thessalonians 5:23 and Hebrews 4:12. The spirit of man is the real essence of man and the part that can contact God and have God-consciousness. However, man also possesses a soul, which is his mind, will, and emotions. The spirit and soul of man is housed in this earth suit, called our body. When a man is born again, his spirit is born into God's Kingdom and is immediately made perfect. However, it is in the soul of man that demons can dwell and exert their evil influence and that sanctification needs to take place.

When I say that "their soul is spread out all over the place," I am referring to their emotions, their thoughts and will being drawn to the other people they've been sexually intimate with. The story I tell a little later in this chapter about the young woman who was unable to feel love for her husband due to previous sexual liaisons is a vivid illustration of what I am saying.

It's one of Satan's biggest hooks for people because he knows that sex was designed by God to be enjoyed between a man and woman in marriage, and sex is primarily spiritual. Satan cannot create; he can only counterfeit or distort. He distorts what God intended for man and woman in the area of sex.

The enemy of our souls works over time to distort our sexuality creating a wealth of demonic entry points. Peter Horrobin, in his book *Healing Through Deliverance*, states that intercourse that does not reflect the divine and spiritual knowing of one partner by another and is nothing but a physical and lustful union, is so far below what God intended for mankind and leaves both persons empty and dissatisfied.

God, in His Word, strongly condemns sexual immorality because He knows it has the power to destroy us both spiritually and physically. It has devastated countless lives, families, communities, and nations. We have only to look at our nation today and see what the sexual revolution of the 1960s has brought into our culture.

The Sexual Tsunami

A recent article in the *American Family Association Journal* entitled "Our Children Are Being Swept Away," refers to a sexual tsunami that has come upon our children. It talks about a hedonistic view of sex that is being spoon fed to our children in many schools, on TV, in the movies, and online. All of these things have their roots in the sexual revolution of the 1960s. According to a Wikipedia article on the subject, the youth rebellion or counterculture which swept our nation in the 1960s brought in a wave of free love and drugs. It had its origin on the college campuses. The youth culture turned abruptly away from the sense of social responsibility and pursued a lifestyle of personal gratification. This cultural rebellion was centered in San Francisco in the Haight-Ashbury district.

The most radical element of this counterculture were the hippies whose sexual revolution challenged conventional mores of sexual behavior. They engaged in drug use and challenged social norms in the area of religion, music, art, and living arrangements. They rejected the mainstream and followed the dictates of Timothy Leary. As former hippies grew older, the 1960s counterculture was absorbed by the mainstream. It left a lasting impact on morality.

Recent surveys taken by religious organizations show that one in four teenage girls ages fourteen to nineteen has a sexually transmitted disease. The number of teens having babies out of wedlock is staggering. Should we be surprised when what was once considered immoral is now blatantly displayed on TV, movies, and magazines? The psalmist in Psalm 12:8 wrote, "What is vile is honored among men." Nothing is truer than what is prominently "honored" and displayed through the media today. Awards are given and licentiousness is esteemed. It is nothing more than glorification of sexual immorality. It is hard to even open a newspaper without seeing half-naked models splashed all over the pages. Our society revels in sex, exalting the virtues of free love. As someone said, free love isn't free. Love, free of responsibility, isn't love at all. It's enslavement, meting out lifelong punishment on those willing to embrace its empty promises of fulfillment and happiness.

I ministered to a young lady who'd been a Christian for many years. Before becoming a Christian, however, she'd slept with too many men to even remember. What she was doing was not only acting out some ancestral patterns, but also trying to establish that father bond that had never been established when she was a child due to an emotionally distant and abusive father.

After I took her through renunciation of those sins, I broke the soul ties between her and all of her many sex partners; when I commanded all of their curses and demons to go back to them, there was strong manifestation. After that I released, by the power of the Holy Spirit, all the parts of their soul back to them; I called back all the parts of her soul from them. Again there was strong physical manifestation during all of that. She said she felt such tremendous release when we were done. When I saw her in church the following Sunday, she told me that for the first time she could actually feel love for her husband and was no longer dreaming of old boyfriends. She felt whole for the first time. There'd been a lot of people in that marriage, not just the two of them!

When I ministered to a gentleman who'd been into drugs and had gotten into pornography and lots of sexual perversion with different women, I did the same thing. His whole body turned beet red, and he started sweating as though he were in a sauna. He was in actual pain in his entire body as we released those demons and curses back to the various women and also parts of their soul. In fact, that part of the ministry was more powerful than the casting out of the demonic from the drugs.

Soul Ties and Abuse

What is the definition of a soul tie? A soul tie is a cleaving together, a relationship whereby two souls are joined or knitted together and in a sense become as one. It is a relationship in which we are either rightfully bonded to someone or subject to bondage. The word "bond" (bonded and bonding) means a rightful and healthy relationship, and the word bondage indicates a relationship that is unhealthy. A soul tie is a bonding (good or bad) that holds people into a relationship whether they like it or not. As a general rule, godly soul ties are God's provision for healthy nurturing and for relationships throughout life, whereas ungodly soul ties will lead to sickness and demonization.

When people are abused, an ungodly soul tie is established between the abuser and the abused. This acts as a demonic tube along which the demonic may transfer from one person to the other. This is especially the case if there has been an emotional or sexual bonding between the abuser and abused.

All abusive relationships result in the formation of ungodly soul ties—whether the abuse is from parents or spouses—be it rejection, physical, verbal or emotional abuse, or ungodly domination and control.

An ungodly marriage relationship will inevitably lead to parent-child ties that will have an ungodly element with them, and there is likely to be more bondage than bonding between the parents and children. God never created us to be abused; if someone stays in an abusive marriage because of legalism or pride or denial, they're not honoring God or helping their children.

One of the things I've discovered is that sexual sin in the bloodline opens the door for female problems in all the succeeding generations. One young lady we ministered to was set free from severe menstrual problems after a spirit of whoredom was cast out of her. She herself had not been sexually promiscuous, but her bloodline had.

TRANSFERENCE

There are many who minister deliverance and do not forbid the demons from transferring to any living being or anywhere down the bloodline; they simply cast them out. That is a very dangerous thing to do. I have seen the reality of that with an incident that happened. Everything I teach in my ministry sessions is from years of experience and the mistakes I've seen others make or that I've made when I was young in the ministry.

Many years ago, before I started my deliverance ministry, I was watching the two-year-old daughter of a woman for whom I had scheduled a deliverance session with two women here in Phoenix. This woman had a history of great rebellion and was in need of much deliverance.

When the little girl awakened from her nap, I took her out of her playpen and put her on the floor. This little girl, who was normally the sweetest child you'd ever want to meet, had a very violent look on her face. She went to a very heavy wooden rocking horse and picked it up and threw it across the room. It was superhuman strength that caused her to do that. She could not, in her own strength, have picked up that heavy wooden rocking horse and thrown it the way she did. I was stunned, but I immediately recognized it as the same spirit that was in her mother. Her mother had a spirit of violence and abuse in her. She had been abused as a child and now was an abuser to her husband.

Apparently the women who were doing deliverance on the mother did not forbid those demons of violence and abuse from transferring down her bloodline. So they did! When they are cast out, they will transfer to the next vessel in the bloodline, unless forbidden from doing so. That is one of the major reasons I forbid demons from transferring down the bloodline of the client I am ministering to. It is also the reason I command those demons to go to the pit.

Now there are some who debate whether or not we have authority to cast demons to the pit. The scripture they use in their argument is Luke 8:27–33 and Mark 5: 1–17, the story of the Gaderene demoniac, which I've covered at great length in another chapter. They will then say that even Jesus didn't send them to the pit when the demons pleaded with Him not to but rather into the herd of swine or pigs, which He did. Let's remember a key component to that incident. When Jesus asked, "What is your name?" the demon answered, "My name is Legion, and we are many." When we look at the fact that a legion of soldiers was anywhere from 4,200 to 6,000 soldiers, it's easy to understand why Jesus would grant them their request. Anyone who's been in deliverance for any length of time knows that when people are heavily demonized, it can be a very long, drawn out battle; many times, strong demons try to cause the maximum amount of pain to the person they're exiting. I can only imagine what a struggle would ensue in casting out 4,000 to 6,000 demons. They seemingly were much more willing to go out of the man if they were allowed to enter into another living being, which would not likely have been the case if they were consigned to the pit.

I have personally seen the reality of this scenario acted out hundreds of times, as demons would plead with me, "Please don't send me to the pit. You don't know how horrible it is down there." Or, "Can I go into his dog or cat?" Or, "Oh, oh, I'm in trouble now!"

TRANSFERENCE
AT DEATH

Death is a time of great spiritual activity and transition. When someone dies, their body becomes an empty shell. The person that was in that body is gone, as our body is only the house for our spirit and soul. When you look into a coffin, you see only the empty shell of the person you once knew. For the Christian, the Bible tells us in 2 Corinthians 5:8, that once we're departed from our body, we are immediately present with the Lord, that is those of us who belong to the Lord Jesus Christ and confess him as our Lord and Savior. A Christian's spirit, in a heartbeat, moves through the invisible veil between the natural world and the spiritual world; they are immediately in heaven, in the presence of their Lord and Savior.

For those who have rejected Christ the Savior, the Bible tells us there is an eternal darkness whereby they are denied the presence of God. That place is called hell. As I explain in the chapter "Heaven or Hell?" God never created hell for mankind, but if people choose to deny Christ and serve the devil instead, there's not much that can be done. God has given us a free will.

There was a group of doctors and nurses who got together and wrote a book in which they documented the dying moments of hundreds of patients under their care. I remember hearing them interviewed on Christian Television, but, unfortunately, don't remember the title of the book. They came to the unanimous conclusion that for the Christian, their dying moments are always sweet and joyous, and they said that invariably the dying Christian will say, "Oh, they're here for me. The holy ones are here to take me home," meaning the angels. There was a stark contrast between the Christians and non-Christians on their deathbed. They said that the non-Christians were filled with fear, and some described some dark beings coming to get them, and they'd cry out with their last breath, "Don't take me. I don't want to go. Somebody help me!"

Death is not only a time of transition for the person who died, as the end of life on this earth has come for them, but it also is a time of transition and great spiritual activity for the demons or unclean spirits which their bodies housed. So the question arises, "What happens to those unclean spirits that just lost their home?" Since they're of the spirit realm, they never die, and because they are living entities, you can clearly see that a dead body would be utterly useless to a demon. Being disembodied spirits, they will immediately seek to occupy a human or animal body as second choice. While they can exist outside of a body, their preference is to be in a human body in order to act out their vile character. For instance, a demon of addiction or murder cannot carry out his vile behavior outside of a human host.

If they have a legal right to the bloodline of the person who just died, they will usually transfer down the bloodline to the next generation. When there is no one in the bloodline to transfer to, the unclean spirits will transfer to someone who has close soul ties to the person who died. They will use those soul ties as a conduit to get into the next vessel. They may also try to transfer to another vessel that is the most similar to the deceased vessel (preferably in the blood line), but if not, then someone who is very much like that person.

If none of the above is available, they hang around, waiting and strategizing and tempting someone to "open" a door through sin so they can then enter into that vessel. Demons cannot act out their ugly nature outside of a human body; their second choice is an animal. I will give you real life case histories to prove my point.

First, I want to address another issue, and that's transference of unclean spirits if you visit a hospital or work in a hospital. What happens in hospitals? People die, don't they? If the unclean spirits that were in the people who just passed away don't have anyone in the bloodline to transfer to, they will then look for an opening in the nurses or doctors working there. I've heard the reality of that with someone who is a part of my ministry. This gentleman has a daughter who is the head of nurses in the hospital. She has had spirits transfer to her with bizarre manifestations after patients pass away. I've instructed her to cleanse herself when she leaves work to forbid any unclean spirits from following her home. She has been doing that and is noticing the difference. We are not to live in any fear or paranoia but simply use wisdom and be aware of the unseen, very real spirit world around us and do the necessary warfare.

Let's look at some case histories which bear out what I've just laid out: When I first got saved, I was in an Assembly of God Church, and the pastor told of a woman being delivered of a spirit of suicide. At the very moment it went out of her, her husband was driving with their beautiful German Shepherd in the back of their pickup truck, and the dog jumped out of the truck and got killed. The dog had driven in that pickup truck for years and years and never once tried to get out. What had happened is that the pastor who was doing deliverance didn't know to cover that woman, her loved ones, their animals, and possessions in the blood of Jesus and to forbid those spirits from transferring to any living being, which is what we at Isaiah 61 do methodically. That unclean spirit transferred to their beloved dog. Is it real? Oh, yes, more real than what we can see and touch!

There is also the case of a young woman who'd come through Isaiah 61 Ministries and been healed and delivered of panic attacks, extreme rage, etc. Well, she was very close to her grandmother who had rescued her and her siblings every time there was chaos in their home from the dad's drunkenness. She also had the same name as her grandmother and looked like her.

One day she went to visit her grandmother who was dying in the hospital. While she was there, her grandmother actually died, but she was resuscitated again and lived for several months after that. When this young woman went home, she found herself feeling sick. She called me the next day and told me she was extremely nauseated, couldn't breathe, and felt like she was dying. I immediately asked her where she'd been the day before.

When she told me about her grandmother, I knew that her grandmother's unclean spirits had transferred the moment she "died." So we did phone deliverance, and she threw up violently but was immediately healed. She then told me that what she had been feeling was exactly what her grandmother was experiencing before she died and was resuscitated. This was a graphic case of demons in the bloodline transferring to the next generation upon the death of one generation. Since they had never been renounced in the grandmother, they had a legal right to transfer. We see they will do so to someone who has strong soul ties to the person passing.

The following story is also told in the chapter "Generational Curses," but because there's a two-fold dimension to what happened to this thirteen year old, I am re-telling it in this chapter. Demons can transfer in the womb. They are then generational demons, and/or they can transfer at the death of a family member. Probably both happened to this young girl.

I talked to a woman in California who was concerned about her daughter. This was a lovely Christian family and home. She went on to tell me that since her young daughter turned thirteen, she'd been having all sorts of irrational fears about being raped. I immediately told her that someone in the bloodline was probably raped, and there was a demon of rape and fear of rape operating in her young daughter. She immediately confirmed what I had just told her. She said that yes, indeed, her grandmother had been raped and actually married the man who raped her which led to years of an abusive and dysfunctional marriage. At that point, I then asked her if her daughter looked like the grandmother that had been raped, and she told me she did. In fact, she said they were going to name her after the grandmother.

I also asked her at that point if the grandmother was deceased, and she told me she had died a few years ago. At which point, I was able to explain to her how demons transfer upon death, also the fact that they look for a vessel that is most like the vessel that just died. She then asked if it could skip a generation, since it had not manifested in her at all. I assured her that generational curses can indeed skip a generation.

When people die, demons don't. They are completely unaffected by the death of their host. Yes, they have to leave the body but are then free to carry on their work in someone else whom they will try to occupy. As stated before, demons are disembodied spirits who need to be in a human body to act out their ugly nature. For example, a demon of alcohol or rage or child abuse cannot act out those things when it is outside of a human body. They are living, functioning, spiritual beings with a mind, personality, and will of their own that are dedicated to the service of Satan.

MULTIPLE PERSONALITIES

Let's look at another aspect of the deliverance we do at Isaiah 61 Ministries, and that's inner healing. Without inner healing, deliverance is just a waste of time; demons are like rats, they love garbage. Unless that emotional garbage is first taken care of, the demons that entered in through that wounding will re-enter the person very quickly.

Many deliverance ministries just go after demons, completely ignoring the root causes of how some of those demons got in. For instance, if you just go after a demon of rebellion, you're just going after the fruit and not getting the root. The root of every demon of rebellion or rebellious behavior is rejection. That rejection either started in the womb—was passed on from Mom or Dad or other ancestors—or came in as a result of what went on in the home as the person was growing up. In order to truly deliver that person, we have to find out what happened in their home relationships with the primary authority figures in their lives. Were Mom and Dad loving and affirming? Did they let the child know he was loved and wanted, or was the message given that he was a nuisance and not really wanted?

Or worse yet, did Mom or Dad tell him he was no good, he'd never amount to anything, or if it wasn't for him, they'd be free to do such and such? If that was the case, a deep root of rejection comes in and is internalized. Later when he grows up, it will show up in self-destructive, rebellious behavior such as drugs, alcohol, promiscuity, etc. He's living out the life script that was given to him by Mom and Dad.

The first thing I have trained my ministry workers to do in interviewing the person whom they're going to minister to is ask the question: "What was your relationship with your mom and dad?" What happens to us as children results in life-long wounds. In his book *Broken Children, Grownup Pain*, Paul Hegstrom says that when there are unresolved traumas from childhood, we will often struggle with unacceptable behavior, such as how we deal with anger, rejection, love, accountability, and authority. Just as would be the case with any untreated physical wound, so it goes with emotional wounds. When left unaddressed, the pain deepens and complications develop in many areas of our personalities and lives.

Depending on the severity of the trauma that has occurred in childhood, there will be either arrested development, which means that we may have grown chronologically, but our emotions are frozen in childhood. We are therefore stunted in areas of our maturity. Or there will be a condition known as multiple personality disorder (MPD) or dissociative identity disorder (DID). If the latter is the case, what happens is that a part of the child's personality has splintered off at the time of trauma. Because the fragile mind and psyche of the child cannot process and deal with the pain inflicted, another personality is formed that will then hold on to the exact details of the trauma—including all the pain, guilt, shame, rejection, and so forth. This part of the personality goes into hiding. This happens so that the core personality can go on with some semblance of normalcy. Basically, it is a fragmentation of the personality. People suffering from MPD usually endured devastating traumas in childhood—such as incest, abuse, etc. Their minds were shattered by feelings of guilt, shame, terror, fear, etc. These emotions, along with the need to survive in the presence of dangerous circumstances, caused them to subconsciously divide their minds into these multiple personalities or "alter personalities."

Children can't run from abuse. The only place they can hide is inside their heads. The alter personality is created to absorb the emotional anguish and physical pain of the trauma. Unfortunately, not only is the mind splintered or the personality fragmented, but a demon also jumps on board to compound the pain.

I ministered to a man whom I'll call Ron for the sake of anonymity, whose wife found our ministry. He said when he first came to one of my deliverance services he was thinking, "Just another thing that won't work." Ron had been to many different treatment centers for multiple personalities—one in California that was very expensive, yet he had found no help. He'd been through everything that the church had to offer—counseling, standing on the Word, etc. He had gone to Christian psychologists, worldly psychologists, psychiatrists, etc., yet had found no help.

Ron was an extremely gifted and intelligent man who was a former Hollywood writer for different TV programs like *Love Boat* and *Hart to Hart*. He'd written books on financial success. He had a degree in law. Ron miraculously survived a childhood that would have driven most people into a mental institution.

He was beaten every day of his life by a despicably sadistic father and by an equally cruel mother and grandmother. He told how one day as an eight-year-old, he hid in the closet because he was so fearful of his dad coming home. His mother found him and began beating him on the head with a frying pan. His grandmother came along and handed the mother an iron and said, "Use this." The stories of abuse he shared with me were horrifying. He was ordered by his dad to beat up another boy on the playground every day of his school life. If he didn't do what he'd been ordered, he'd be severely beaten by his dad at the end of the day. He lived in constant terror.

As a result of this constant fear and terror in his life, he had many, many multiple personalities. They were all different ages, corresponding to the ongoing traumas in his life. He also had many, many demons that had jumped on board all those traumas. He told how one of his personalities had completely memorized the Bible, but he, the core Ron, did not know the Bible that well. One of his personalities knew the answer to very complicated math problems almost immediately without using paper to figure it out. He graduated from law school, but he did not remember much of what he'd learned, although there was a personality hidden within him that memorized all the law books. It went on and on. When I first started ministering to him, I never knew which personality I was talking to.

After dealing with and healing a few of his multiple personalities, he was so grateful that he said we should really capture the process on video camera in order to help others with similar problems. I agreed, and the next session we had a video camera set up to film the session. He sat in the chair and said, "What's the camera for?" I told him we were going to film the session as per our last conversation. He said, "Oh no, I'm not into that," and he wouldn't let us film it. It was this sort of thing that was driving his wife crazy.

He also said after he married his first wife, he got to the hotel room after the wedding and looked at her and thought, "Who is that, and why is she here with me?" Sound bizarre? It's true.

This is what multiple personalities are like. His was an extreme case because of the severe trauma he'd endured as a child.

Well, after ministering to him for about five months, just once a week for a couple of hours, Ron is a whole man. He said that for the first time in his life, he doesn't feel like he's just in the background observing, rather he is finally living and feeling life. He'd always before felt like someone else was doing all those things, and he was totally distanced and detached from what was going on. He'd had probably forty different personalities and hundreds of demons that had attached themselves to the different childhood traumas and terror.

With multiple personalities, we have them ask Jesus into their hearts, and then have Jesus heal them of the wounding. Once they are healed, we integrate them into the person's core personality so that person can become the man or woman of God that God created him/her to be—healed and whole. Then we cast out the demons that jumped on board those wounds, and the healing is complete. It works every time. I am so grieved when I read in different deliverance books that there is no such thing as multiple personalities or alter personalities, that it's just demons. I could give you case after case of people with alter personalities who were completely healed after going through this process.

There is another very interesting story about multiple personalities that I just have to share with you. This happened when I was rather young in the ministry. A woman was brought into my ministry who was severely abused as a child—physically, emotionally, and sexually.

She knew that she had multiple personalities because she would talk to her "little children," as she called them. They each had different ages and different names. She had a five-year-old called Ruthie who was sexually abused by her daddy. She also had two boy personalities. They were boy alters (which simply means alter personalities) because she felt that if she was a boy they might not have hurt her. The boys were Danny, who was fourteen years old, and Michael, who was ten years old. I ministered healing to all of those personalities and incorporated them into her core personality.

She then told me about a very mean young adult personality named Virginia, and how she was always afraid that Virginia might surface because of the terrible things she did. She said she'd gone to a psychiatrist, and he called Virginia up. She started to tear up his office, and he ran out of there and locked her in and called the police.

Needless to say, I had great trepidation in calling Virginia up, yet I knew that in order for this woman to be healed, Virginia had to accept Jesus and be integrated into her core personality. So with great trepidation, I called Virginia up. Wow, she came up and starting cussing, and said, "I'm getting out of here," with a few choice expletives, of course. I posted angels on either side of this woman and told the angels to hold her in the chair. Well, they did exactly that. As she tried to get out of the chair, she found she couldn't move.

Leading her to receive Jesus as Lord and Savior was the next challenge. She said arrogantly, "Why would I do that? Me—I just want men, sex, and drugs." The Holy Spirit gave me the right words to say. I challenged her to try Jesus. I said to her, "You may think you have everything you want, but you don't have one thing. And that's *peace*. Jesus is the only one who can give you that." She said, "Peace? What's peace?" Then I explained what peace was, and she hesitantly said, "Well, I guess I can try, but it better work or else..." So I had her ask Jesus into her heart and immediately asked the Holy Spirit to integrate Virginia into this woman's core personality. The integration was powerful. This woman, whom I'll call Lydia, went from having this mean, nasty look on her face, to an almost angelic countenance. Then when it was done, Lydia was back, and I told her that Virginia was now also integrated and gone. She couldn't believe it. So I challenged her to call Virginia up, which she was fearful of doing, but she finally did. She was gone!

I talked to her a week later and asked her how she was doing. She said she couldn't believe it. For the first time in her life she was able to concentrate and really function because she didn't have all these voices in her head telling her different things. She said it was so peaceful. Then I talked to her after more time passed, and she told me that she was finally able to succeed in business because she could now function as a whole human being and not this splintered person who was fragmented and confused.

It is a very, very real thing, and God's children should not be going to the world for help. They should be able to find this type of help right in the Body of Christ. She'd been a Christian for most of her life yet had not received the freedom she needed until now. She also had a lot of demons that jumped on board all the child abuse, which we also took care of.

As Christians, in order to live a fulfilled and abundant life, we need to appropriate all that Christ came to give us! We received forgiveness for our sins when we asked Christ into our lives, but we now need to be delivered from the consequences of those sins. Forgiveness does not automatically include deliverance from the penalty but rather is a separate benefit that needs to be appropriated. Forgiveness is only part one of the package. The full package contains deliverance from what the enemy has done in our lives and in our bloodline.

Another woman who needed this type of help was a prophetic lady minister. She was someone who was strongly being used of God in the prophetic and was ministering in different churches. She was also one who was not even aware that she had multiple personalities. She'd just come back from ministering in a church in Florida and felt like some kind of witchcraft transferred to her, so I set up an appointment to go minister to her.

I went to the appointment with the idea that we'd just take care of the witchcraft and be done. Well, it turned into two or three different sessions with her. She was from South America and had been abused by her mother. When I started to call up a demon of witchcraft, which is what I thought we were going to deal with, all of a sudden she went into an alter personality.

She became a little girl and started twirling her skirt around her finger like a little girl would do and swinging her legs back and forth under the chair. I was amazed. I healed the little girl from the things that were done to her, integrated her into the woman's core personality, and cast out the demons that were in her from all the victimization. She'd been taken to witchdoctors many times by her mother when she was a little girl, so I had her renounce all of that and cast out the demons that entered through that open door.

She also had been sexually molested by her brother as a little girl while his friends watched, and it caused her such shame that she still carried it into adulthood. She told me that she could never go into public restrooms because she was so afraid that someone would look under the stall door and see her. Even in the privacy of her own home, she would always stuff a towel under the bathroom door to be sure no one could see her. She was finally set free from all that torment through the inner healing and deliverance.

Can you see how many good people are being tormented by the demonic because they've been told that a Christian couldn't possibly have a demon? She'd been carrying all this torment around all of her life, and she was now in her forties serving Christ as a full time minister.

EMOTIONAL INNER HEALING

What I and other valid deliverance ministries have discovered is that the most important aspect of deliverance is not simply the casting out of demons but rather the emotional healing which most often opened the door for the demons. Since they ride in on emotional wounding or trauma, if it is not taken care of first, the demons will be very strong and put up much resistance. There is also the fact that it was the wounding and trauma that gave them their legal right to be there in the first place. Barring the necessary emotional inner healing, you will have a very difficult deliverance session that will drag on for hours with little or no success. Oh, one or two demons may eventually leave just to get away from the harassment, leaving the person feeling good for a little bit. But they will quickly become re-infested, as their legal rights have not been broken, and the emotional garbage is still in the person. As I said before, demons are like rats. They feed on garbage—emotional garbage!

The casting out of demons without the necessary emotional healing has the same effect as putting a bandage on a dirty physical wound. What's bound to happen is that the wound will fester and become seriously infected until that person's life is threatened. We can see that inner healing hand in hand with casting out of demons is the perfect formula. One without the other is utter failure. They go "hand in glove." This applies only to those who've had childhood abuse of any sort or neglect, deep rejection, or trauma. It also holds true for adult abuse.

Another aspect of unhealed emotional wounds is that many infirmities and diseases can be traced to these unhealed emotional wounds and the unhealthy perception they have created in us.

Henry Wright has written a book entitled *A More Excellent Way*. The entire book is devoted to sicknesses, diseases, and infirmities that ride in on unhealed emotions. He says on the subject of self-hate that once the devil has convinced us to not like ourselves, this creates resistance and discord among the white blood cells and antibodies in us. Our autoimmune system is our first line of defense against the invasion of bacteria and disease. Self-hatred allows the enemy to take out the protection and turn the white blood cells against the very tissue they were designed to protect. The physical systems designed to guard and heal us begin to devour us. Their assignments to repair and restore are reversed by the lies we believe about ourselves and the goodness of life. He says that it only makes sense if I hate myself, it is hard to believe that the members of my body would not follow suit.

Let us now look at how some of these emotional wounds occur: As all human beings are born with an innate longing and need to be loved, when a child is deprived of that deep need through bad parenting, a strong root of rejection establishes itself into the very core of that child. Out of that root will come some very undesirable fruit—such as rebellion, self-hate, low self-esteem, addictions, self-destruction, failure, sabotage of any blessings God has for someone, and a whole tangled system of behaviors, all of which will be driven by the demonic. It will create a stronghold in their lives until that stronghold is torn down through the wonderful ministry of inner healing and deliverance.

Since we determine our value by the worth our parents have placed on us, if they hurt us deliberately through any form of abuse or subjected us to neglect, we will then conclude that we must be inferior and unlovable. Childhood is a time when the parents have the awesome responsibility of creating their child's self-image and self-worth and what he's going to believe about himself throughout his life. How we are treated by our first authority figures in our lives sets the foundation out of which we construct our self-image. We tend to become what we were either told or the message that was conveyed to us by our parents.

If a child has been programmed with low self-esteem or low self-worth, he will likely follow a pattern of failure by putting little value on what he does. He will certainly not try to succeed, or he will go down a different path. That's the path of over-performance, based on the need to prove himself. This performance-driven individual will, even at the height of his success, always have a deep, nagging feeling of inadequacy and unworthiness, freezing up at the slightest rejection or criticism.

The child who has been programmed with low self-esteem and unworthiness may never reach his full potential, the plans that God has for His life. In my view, the more devastating consequence of having that kind of childhood programming is that person's inability to receive God's love. After all, how could God love us if our parents couldn't?

Once we become adults and become a child of God, we need to take a formal review of the belief systems that have been ingrained into us in childhood. What our earthly parents told us, if it was not loving and nurturing, is from the devil, and they were led of the devil to destroy and cripple us for life with wrong belief systems. The good news is that we can cast off those wrong beliefs about ourselves and begin to reprogram ourselves with what God says about us.

What are just some of the things God the Father says to us and about us?

1. You are made in His image. (Genesis 1:27)

2. You are his offspring. (Acts 17:28)

3. He chose us when He planned creation. (Ephesians 1:11–12)

4. We are not a mistake. (Psalm 139:15–16)

5. You are fearfully and wonderfully made. (Psalm 139:14)

6. God knit you together in your mother's womb. (Psalm 139:13)

7. God desires to lavish His love on you. (1 John 3:1)

8. God offers you more than your earthly father ever could. (Matthew 7:11)

9. God is the perfect father. (Matthew 5:48)

10. God's plan for your future is filled with hope. (Jeremiah 29:11)

11. God rejoices over you with singing. (Zephaniah 3:17)

12. You are God's treasured possession. (Exodus 19:5)

13. One day God will wipe away every tear from your eyes. (Revelation 21:3–4)

14. When you are broken-hearted, God is close to you. (Psalm 34:18)

These are just some of the hundreds of words of love that God our Father has for us in the Bible. This is who you *really* are.

Getting back to damaged children, we see that much of what we are today is the result of our childhood, whether good or bad. Of course, there is also the matter of ancestral/generational curses passed down the bloodline, but right now we are looking at inner healing. What happens to us in childhood (as stated above) results in our either growing up to be secure, confident adults who know how to love and be loved—that is if we had parents who were godly and nurtured and valued us. If you were one who was blessed with that kind of home environment, you should be praising the Lord every day of your life. You should also let your parents know how grateful you are. However, for those who were raised in a home where the parents were immature, selfish, abusive, or neglectful, creating a dysfunctional environment that was more like a battle zone rather than a place of security, then that is not going to be the case.

A very problematic adulthood will also result from those that were raised in alcoholic or drug addicted families. That kind of home environment is going to produce children who are going to be extremely emotionally wounded and, consequently, very insecure. They are going to view everything in their adult life through the prism of the dysfunction they experienced in their homes as they were growing up.

A very handsome gentleman, who had miraculously survived an incredibly abusive childhood, told me he couldn't stand to look in the mirror. He said he would start to feel sick every time he saw himself in the mirror or in pictures. He couldn't stand to see a picture of himself. No matter what the mirror showed or what others told him, he felt like he was extremely ugly. He saw himself through the prism of his abusive childhood and what his authority figures did to him. It was only after some deep inner healing for those wounds and the casting out of demons of self-hatred that he was able to look in the mirror and see himself as others saw him.

If these childhood issues are not addressed, they result in lifelong wounds that will bleed over into every arena of that person's life and relationships. A husband that, coming from an abusive childhood, has not received the necessary healing and deliverance will then subject his wife to sudden episodes of irrational anger, bringing the marriage into jeopardy. Or the reverse can be true. It could be the wife! Because that inner reservoir of childhood hurt and pain has been pushed down, stuffed in, and a lid has been put on it, it will bubble up and boil over at the slightest incident. They've built their marriage on a rotten foundation, a foundation of suppressed hurt and pain, which will eventually erode the marriage. Imagine for a moment what kind of a building contractors would build if they didn't clear the ground first by removing all the rubble or if they tried to lay the foundation on a swamp without first draining and cleaning up the swamp.

It has been my experience that a wife who has been sexually molested as a child by either her father, foster father, or boyfriend of the mother will, many times not be able to enjoy sex with her husband, or may become very promiscuous. I have seen both. I've ministered to many, many women for whom this had been a major problem in marriage. However, with inner healing and deliverance that can all be turned around.

A child's mind is not capable of processing severe trauma and resultant emotional wounds. Emotional wounds, like untreated physical wounds, will cause complications; there will be lifelong ramifications. A physical bruise is caused by inner bleeding. An emotional wound is also caused by inner bleeding, i.e. bleeding of the heart.

Let me give you an example of what I was saying regarding unresolved childhood issues. I ministered to a woman years ago who was in her seventies and had been a Christian all of her life. A friend of hers brought her to my ministry. She came wanting to be set free from extreme arthritis. She came in limping. Her right knee had extreme arthritis, as well as her hands.

As I interviewed her, I found that she still had issues from childhood when her mother was abusive to her. Those things had never been resolved, and she was still hanging on to the pain, which then led to bitterness. To look at her, you'd never believe she had bitterness operating in her. She was a sweet Christian lady.

I knew immediately that the bitterness and inability to forgive was causing the arthritis. I led her in a prayer of forgiveness of her mother and then ministered inner healing to that little girl who'd been abused. Then I proceeded to cast out the spirits of child abuse, pain, inability to forgive, and bitterness. As they left, her arthritis was immediately healed. Her fingers straightened out, and her knee was immediately healed. She was so elated that she said she felt like dancing.

Lets look at some of the results of being raised in a dysfunctional home, with either abusive parents or parents who were too busy with their own selfish pursuits and battles to nurture and love their children, or in an alcoholic home are:

These are the deficiencies you may see as a result of that type of upbringing:

1. Inability to find genuine relationships or build emotionally intimacy in adulthood.

2. A prevailing feeling of being flawed.

3. Will feel insecure and unworthy. As a result he will sabotage anything good that comes into his life—sabotage the ways that God would try to bless him.

4. Will most likely be childish and self-centered.

5. Will exhibit unacceptable behavior, such as how they deal with anger, rejection, love, accountability, and authority.

6. Will overreact to small irritations.

7. Will experience depression that will be unrelated to present circumstances.

8. Will have nightmares and weird dreams.

9. Will experience strange sleep patterns.

10. Will have self-hate.

11. Will find themselves mired in feelings of inadequacy and self-rejection.

12. Will be unable to receive love from others.

13. Will blame themselves for what happened to them in childhood, since children seem to have that tendency anyway.

14. Will be unable to receive the love of God. After all, our mother/father didn't love us, why would God love us?

15. Will have difficulty in trusting others since the primary authority figures in their lives when they were children (Mom and Dad) could not be trusted.

16. Will usually be controlling, since they grew up in an environment where everything that was happening around them was out of control. They will then, as adults, attempt to control all the people in their lives.

17. Will identify everyone's behaviors as a continuation of the rejection they experienced in childhood causing them to be defensive. They will always take innocent comments personally. Their perspective becomes completely skewed and distorted.

18. Will struggle with self-hatred. A child believes everything parents tell him and is not capable of sorting things out. Therefore if Mom and Dad make him feel he's a mistake or should never have been born through constant rejection or neglect, he'll grow up believing the same thing and have severe self-hatred. (Note: I find that in deliverance sessions on child abuse issues, nearly everyone in the room has a spirit of self-hatred in them, which then leads to self-destruction and self-sabotage. Self-hatred seems to be one of the most common results.)

19. Will have either what is known as arrested development, or if the abuse was severe will have developed Multiple Personality Disorder or Dissociative Identity Disorder.

When we've been abused as children, either physically, mentally, emotionally, or sexually, we'll usually build walls because the trust factor that is built into children has been destroyed by the abusive authority figures in our lives. We'll be afraid to let down those walls and be transparent, fearing that if they really knew us they wouldn't like us. This of course then prohibits us from finding the help we need. Many will live in denial until God breaks through that denial and shows them their need for inner healing.

It's been said that Satan works much like a shark. As long as the shark is in the water, his environment, he is a great threat to us. The minute he is brought out of the water and put on the sand, an environment that is not his own, he loses all power. So it is with Satan and his minions. As long as things are kept in the dark, Satan's environment, he has power and free reign. The minute these issues are brought into the light, the environment of God, Satan loses his hold.

If healing is not brought to some of these childhood issues when that person reaches adulthood, he will tend to be a very defensive and argumentative person, someone who is very hard to get along with. Most of us know people like that—people who are offended by everything. Also if those childhood wounds are not healed, a spirit of bitterness will enter in and begin to control our lives and decisions. We will then make bad decisions out of that bitter spirit, and it will lead us further into destruction. Bitterness is a destructive enemy that will prohibit us from living in abundance and prosperity.

Another sign of untreated childhood wounds are people who are always lashing out at someone. And, of course, it's because they are harboring not only bitterness but also anger and rage because of the injustices they suffered in childhood that have never been addressed.

When we hang onto that anger, rage, and bitterness for any length of time, unclean spirits with those names enter into us. Just about everyone I've ministered deliverance to who had some sort of abusive childhood has had strong spirits of rage and anger and bitterness—even some of the sweetest women you'd ever want to meet. They've just been very good at repressing it and not allowing it to control them.

Overeating is oftentimes a sign of unresolved childhood issues, other times it could be a spirit of gluttony that has been ruling the family line. People who turn to alcohol and drugs are hurting adults who've never received inner healing for their childhood wounds, or it can be a heavy generational curse of alcohol and drugs that they inherited in the womb. They're either going to attempt to anesthetize their pain with drugs or alcohol when the emotional pain becomes unbearable or will turn to food as a source of comfort.

Anorexia or bulimia are also addictions, similar to any other addiction—be it alcohol, drugs, pornography, sex, or whatever. The root of all of these things can be traced to is untreated childhood wounds. Much of it is rejection and self-hate related to a lack of parental love and approval. Unless these things are taken care of, they will pass on to the next generation. Even if you had a heavy bloodline history of addiction to any of the above things and you were able to stand against it and not cave in to the pressure of these generational weaknesses, the next generation may not be able to. Also if it's not broken and cast out of you, it may turn to another form of addiction—the same spirit but causing different problems.

Blame shifting is another sign of an adult bearing scars from an abusive childhood. The wounded person will never take accountability for their mistakes but will always spin the situation in order to escape blame. Another protective mechanism is justification. They will always try to justify their behavior/mistakes, rather than admitting their faults—anything to keep from examining themselves.

If the adult who has come from a dysfunctional family does not receive healing for his childhood wounds what will happen is that they will most likely go into wrong, addictive relationships, which will then become a curse and be passed on to their children. That adult will sometimes go from relationship to relationship looking for someone to fix their wounds when the reality is that only God can fix their wounds and meet their needs.

The biggest problem is that they will usually attract someone who has similar wounds and similar demons, thus creating this addictive relationship and years of pain for the man and woman and greater pain for their children. We know, of course, that demons jump on board childhood wounds, compounding the pain and problems. So the person is not only left with emotional wounds, but there are demons attached to those wounds, making sure that the patterns are repeated in their relationships and family. Those unclean spirits in that person will draw others who will continue the cycle of abuse and unhappiness in their life.

Because they have not received healing for their childhood wounds and deliverance of the unclean spirits attached to the wounds, the couple in an addictive relationship have little to no ability to handle normal relational and family conflicts with any sort of maturity. They can't! Not only because of unhealed wounds and unresolved issues, but also because they have no reference point. Needless to say, they have no ability to raise their children with maturity and love, being too caught up with their own childish behavior and pain.

Unfortunately, a couple in this type of sick relationship will most often stay in it, not only because it's the easy thing to do but many times it's the only thing they've ever known. For someone like that, the fear of the unknown, fear of what the future may hold, and fear of what people might think will keep them chained to that sick relationship. Without inner healing and deliverance, the people in this type of addictive, dysfunctional relationship are so overcome by the darkness that they don't even recognize what's in operation. Pity the poor children who have to endure that type of dysfunction in their home, and I see so many of them. I know it's a miracle of God that they made it through. But, of course, once they accept Jesus as their Lord and Savior, the healing that is so badly needed can come. God is so good; He longs to bless us and restore us. It's only in the kingdom of God that we can be restored to wholeness.

INNER VOWS AND THE POWER OF WORDS

Let's look very briefly at another open door for demonic strongholds in a person's life, and that is the door of inner vows, which I have not yet mentioned.

Inner vows are a very important aspect of the inner healing that we do. I have found that at times when all the inner healing has been done and all the appropriate demons have been cast out and the person is still struggling with an issue, there must be an inner vow involved. That is why deliverance and inner healing are so complex and must be: (a) completely led by the Holy Spirit, and (b) the people doing it must be well trained in all the different aspects of it.

An inner vow is a vow made in anger—usually as a result of some injustice done to us as children. Vows we make currently also affect us, but an inner vow is one set into us as children and then completely forgotten as adults. It is a determination set by the mind and heart into all the being in early life, and our inner being persistently retains this programming, no matter what changes of mind and heart may later occur.

An inner vow resists the normal maturity process and resists change. We do not grow out of them. An inner vow may not kick in until the appropriate time when triggered by the right persons or situations.

Inner vows are very common in children, and they vary in intensity. We can liken an inner vow to a train on a railroad track. No matter which way the engineer may want to go, the train will not change direction unless someone switches tracks. So it is with inner vows. Until those vows are brought into the open and renounced and broken, they will keep us on the same undesirable track. For an example, if a young girl has experienced a lost childhood due to parents who had one baby after another and subsequently had no time or energy to give the young girl the love and attention she so craved, or worse yet, they put upon her the responsibility for taking care of her siblings, she may make an inner vow that when she grows up she won't be like Mom and have babies. At that point, her inner being interprets such a vow as an order not to ever allow pregnancy.

Then when she gets married and longs for babies, she finds she's unable to conceive. If that inner vow is found and renounced and broken, her body will then be able to conceive.

Let me give you a classic case of an inner vow in operation. I ministered to a gentleman who was fifty years old and has been addicted to drugs for thirty-five years of his life. He was an intelligent man—a former college football player and businessman.

This drug addiction would drive him and cause him to self-destruct every time God would try to bless him and things were going well in his life. That was the pattern and stronghold in his life since high school. He would go for about six months, and then he'd fall right back into it.

He had been through every program known to mankind, trying to get rid of this drug addiction. When he finally enrolled in Teen Challenge, he received Jesus Christ as his Lord and Savior and started his Christian walk. However, his addiction was still there, and as soon as he graduated Teen Challenge, he got drawn back into drugs, as much as he tried to resist.

A friend of his who knew about my ministry asked me to minister to him. I ministered several times to him, and he had extremely *strong* deliverances; the demons coming out of him caused his entire body to turn beet red—his legs, his arms, and his face. They roared out of him like a wild bull elephant. However, even though I'd cast out all the right unclean spirits, in about six months he'd be drawn back into drugs. I went into prayer one evening and asked the Holy Spirit to show me what the root of his problem was. The Holy Spirit told me it was an inner vow that he'd made as a boy.

I then told this gentleman what the Lord had shown me and told him to go into prayer and ask the Holy Spirit to show him what that inner vow was. The next day he told me that as soon as he asked, the Holy Spirit said, "Your uncle." This uncle was his dad's older brother, and he, at the time, thought he was the coolest man alive. When he was just twelve years old, his beloved uncle died at the very young age of forty-five of lung cancer. His uncle was a great-looking man, a war veteran, an athlete, but also a smoker and a recovering alcoholic.

He told me that he remembered looking at his uncle in his casket and thought, "I'll die too at forty-five years of age." So with that driving him, he thought, "I may as well party and have fun because I'm going to die anyway."

What was in operation and driving this gentleman to self-destruct was an inner vow he'd made when he looked at his beloved uncle in the casket. That vow opened the way for demons of self-destruction, death, expectation of premature death, recklessness, self-sabotage, and poverty; this set him up every time he'd start to prosper.

I had him renounce and break that inner vow, then I called up that young boy who was so devastated when his uncle died and had him ask Jesus into his heart and ask Jesus to heal him of the grief, pain, etc., and then integrated that young, wounded boy into the man's core personality. Then I went for the demons of self-destruction, death, premature death, recklessness, self-sabotage, and poverty; he experienced a strong inner healing and deliverance. He told me he felt such incredible peace when we were done, and all desire for drugs was now gone.

Inner vows can hold us to a pattern of self-destruction, or whatever the inner vow entailed, like a train is held to a railroad track. Well, we switched the tracks in this man's life! He has finally been set completely free from all desire for drugs!

Inner vows we make as children will then lie, long forgotten, until the right set of circumstances triggers them into action. However, vows we make as adults can be just as harmful and destructive. We can curse ourselves with words such as, "I'll never trust a man again," or "I'm always losing my job," or "I think I'm getting sick." Guess what that does? It releases the invisible spirit world into action to fulfill what we've just spoken over ourselves. When we speak God's Word over us, it releases God's angels to fulfill what we have spoken. When we speak negative things over us, it releases the demonic realm to gladly fulfill what we have spoken over ourselves.

If Christians only realized the power of their words they would weigh each word carefully as the Scriptures admonish us to do. We have the Spirit of God in us. The same Spirit that created the universe by His spoken words lives in us; therefore, we must be *so careful* with the words we speak. In the book of Proverbs, it tells us that "life and death are in the power of the tongue" (Proverbs 18:21). Second Peter 1:4 says that we are "partakers in God's divine nature." If God's nature was such that He spoke and created the universe, surely our words also have a great power to create circumstances. Jesus told us in Matthew 5:37 that we are to let our *yes* be *yes*, our *no* be *no*, and we are not to swear by anything else.

A very tragic example of what can happen as a result of a rash vow is a gentleman I ministered to. He pleaded with me to help him as he was being tormented because of what happened.

He told me that several years before he'd had an adulterous affair, and when his wife confronted him with her suspicions, he swore to her on his son's life that he was not having an affair. His son, twenty years old, was killed in an automobile accident shortly thereafter. Coincidence or consequence? You decide!

Another example of the power of a Christian's words is what happened when I was attending a small Assembly of God Church in Phoenix. I started hearing that many of the women in the congregation had been having miscarriages. This immediately raised a red flag. I suspected some sort of curse in operation, but the mystery wasn't solved until I heard the pastor get up one day and ask for prayer for his daughter-in-law, back in New Zealand, who'd just suffered a miscarriage.

The next time the pastor and I had lunch together, I shared my suspicions with him and asked him a series of questions, trying to get to the bottom of this mystery. As we talked, he shared with me how he had dismissed someone on his staff several years prior. He told me the man was irate and threatened him in a very ominous way. He told him something to the effect of, "You will be sorry. You don't know what you've just done. There will be no new life or growth (I cannot remember the exact choice of words) in your church because of what you've done." That was the answer I was seeking. I told him that basically the man had put a death curse on the church, which apparently was affecting all the new life or pregnancies in the church and had even affected his own family.

He received what I told him, and the next time we were in the church, I stood with him at the front of the church before the service began and had him repeat after me the words for the breaking of that curse of death over the congregation and his own family. Ten months later, he announced that this same daughter-in-law had given birth to a beautiful new baby.

SPIRITS OF INFIRMITY

"Death and life are in the power of the tongue; and they that love it shall eat the fruit thereof" (Proverbs 18:21, KJV)

Do our words carry power? Indeed they do, just as the Bible warns us, and it is more real than you and I can even imagine! I want to expound a bit on the power of our words in regards to infirmity or sickness:

One of the job functions of demons is to bring sickness, and these are "spirits of infirmity." Some spirits of infirmity have very specific conditions that they cause. For example: cancer, paralysis, etc. One of the biggest assignments for Satan's hordes of hell is to bring sickness and poverty to God's people. I will give you a very specific example of spirits of infirmity being laid on God's people in a minute, but first I want to teach you to stand against whatever Satan has assigned to you. Let me explain that more fully.

Suppose there is an epidemic of flu going around. All of a sudden you start to feel symptoms. *Don't receive them.* It is unclean spirits or demons (the Bible uses unclean spirits and demons interchangeably) laying those symptoms on you. Resist them by saying something like, "No, you don't, Satan"—even though it's not Satan personally, it's his demons. We are just letting them know we know who's behind the assignment—"I don't receive your ugly package. Take these lying symptoms and go!" You may have to resist for a while, or sometimes they go immediately, depending on how well you know your authority in Christ. Remember, possession is ninety-nine percent of the law. Once it's in you, it's harder to get out. So stand against it as soon as you feel symptoms.

You see, demons recognize those who know their authority, and they fear and tremble when such a person speaks. Anyone who has Jesus Christ as their Lord and Savior has authority over unclean spirits. Didn't Jesus say "He who believes in Me, the works that I do shall he do also; and greater works than these shall he do..." (John 14:12, NAS)?

Walking in Authority

Let me give you a few examples of this, and this is only a few of hundreds I could give you. One morning when I awakened and looked in the mirror after washing my face, I noticed a sty had appeared out of nowhere at the corner of my left eye. I remembered that my mother had rather large sty in the very same corner of her left eye all of her life. It was very unsightly, and I often wondered why she'd not had it removed.

Well, I knew immediately what was in operation here. It was a generational curse. I went to work and immediately broke the generational curse and then laid hands on that sty and commanded it to leave. The next time I looked in the mirror, it was completely gone. Then a few weeks later, the very same scenario. I immediately said, "No, you don't, Satan. Take your ugly package and go." Again, the next time I looked in the mirror it was completely gone.

There have been numerous times that the demonic world has tried to lay various ailments upon me. As soon as I would feel a certain symptom, I would actively resist, and it would leave. Sometimes it would be a very strong assignment, and it would take more warfare than other times. Believe me; it is well worth the effort. I am a walking, talking testimony of the effectiveness of this. I walk in divine health and never get the colds, flu, or viruses that are "going around."

Do you remember the headlines in the newspapers, as we headed toward winter one year, about a big epidemic of bird flu that was supposed to hit our nation? Well, when I saw that, I laid hands on the newspaper headline and cast that demonic prophesy to the ground and forbid it from being fulfilled. Then when I met with my prayer warriors later in the week, I had them pray with me. Guess what? It never happened! Jesus said, "Behold, I give unto you power to tread on serpents and scorpions, and over all the power of the enemy, and nothing shall by any means hurt you" (Luke 10:19, KJV). Serpents and scorpions refer to Satan's dark angels and demons.

When I first came into the knowledge of deliverance, there was a young man doing deliverance out of his home. I had gone there to help a lady from my church get her son delivered. Her son never showed up. Having just read in a deliverance book that allergies were unclean spirits and because I had contracted severe environmental allergies since moving to Phoenix, I asked him to minister to me. Well, he cast the allergy spirits out, and for the first time I was able to sleep through the night without getting up and taking my naturopathic allergy medi-cation. What a blessing that was! The symptoms used to be so severe that I'd wake up several times during the night feeling like my head was about to explode from the pressure.

I was so elated that I couldn't wait to call him in the morn-ing. When I did call him, he said they had transferred to him, and he'd struggled all night with allergy symptoms. He did not know, nor did I, to forbid those spirits from transferring. Unfortunately, our ignorance can cost us greatly at times.

For two glorious months I was completely free from allergies, and then one night, when I was extremely exhausted, I awoke in the middle of the night with familiar allergy symptoms. Demons don't play fair. They will always attack when you're exhausted or are dealing with all kinds of problems. This was before I knew to do spiritual warfare and cleanse my room and seal it in the blood of Jesus every night. Prior to that I would get attacked on a regular basis, and it was always at night.

Through the Holy Spirit's direction, I have come up with a Dream Covering and Insomnia Covering, which is really protection covering for the night. I include that in the back of this book.

Well, when I was awakened with the familiar symptoms, the first thought that came into my head was, *There's still some allergy medication in the medicine cabinet. Why not just go and take it?* Then I realized who was putting those thoughts into my head, and I started to rebuke those symptoms, as tired as I was. It took a while, but they finally left and have never returned. It was certainly worth losing a couple of hours of sleep to retain my deliverance.

There is another specific example of how spirits of infirmity are assigned to God's people. One Sunday evening as I finished up a group deliverance at the church where I held our deliverance services, I noticed a disturbance at the back of the sanctuary. I went back there to see what was happening.

There was a lady standing up, and I could see the obvious strong demon that had taken her over. She had been brought to the deliverance service by a friend. One of my deliverance ministers was trying to deal with that demon, but it was so strong that they couldn't get anywhere with it.

I was extremely exhausted from ministering steadily for three hours. I did not feel like dealing with another single demon but had no choice since no one could do anything with this demon, and we had to lock up the church. In a situation like that, when we are out of time, I will simply bind up the demon and command it to go back down until a later date when we have time to deal with it.

The anointing upon my life for deliverance is very strong, and it came at great cost. But never had I dealt with a demon that wouldn't obey my commands up until that point! When I said, "I have authority over you, you foul spirit, now I command you to obey and go down," it started mocking me. It wasn't until afterwards that I found out why it was so disobedient. In talking with her friend who had brought her to the ministry, I found out that this woman was living in open sin. She was living with a man and had many children out of wedlock, and none of that had been confessed. She had lots of other sin in her life.

Usually when the vessel is walking in disobedience to God's word and ways, the demons in them will be disobedient since they know they have a right to be there. We weaken demons by walking in obedience to God's Word and ways, asking forgiveness for sins, and forgiving others. This woman had done none of the above; therefore, her demons had total control of her.

When the demon was up and speaking through this woman, as a weakening technique, I told him that Jesus had defeated his master, Satan; therefore, he had to obey. At that, he pointed to all the people still in the room, and said, "Ha! Then how come we have all these people?" I needed to find out what he meant by that and commanded him to tell me how he had all these people. He laughed and said, "We put infirmity on every one of them." That's what they do, folks! Infirmity and poverty are the two big spirits being put on God's people, and because of lack of knowledge of the demonic realm and how they operate, we think it's God's will. "My people are destroyed for lack of knowledge" (Hosea 4:6, NKJV). Of course, he ultimately had to obey the commands of the servant of the Lord, but it confirmed what I already knew, that demons are behind most infirmity, sickness, and disease.

Another case history of infirmity being put on someone is what happened to my daughter Lisa. This is yet another example of how spirits of infirmity can operate. When she had graduated from Oral Roberts University, she came over one day (she was living on her own at this point). To my horror, I saw that two knuckles on her right hand that were very bruised and red/purple and swollen. I asked her what happened. She told me that it was nothing. It was the knuckles she used to hit her brother with. It was their way of "horsing around." I didn't think much about it.

A few days later she came over again. This time all of the knuckles on her right hand were swollen, purple, and bruised. Now even she looked alarmed. I asked her if I could pray over them, and she allowed me to. Nothing changed. Her condition only got worse despite my laying hands on her and claiming healing about three different times.

Well, one Saturday afternoon, I had just come home from street evangelizing with my church, and the Holy Spirit was strongly on me. She was over again, and I asked if I could pray over her one more time. She said, "It didn't work the last few times." But she finally allowed me to.

What happened after that completely amazed both of us. As I laid hands on her knuckles, I said things I had no way of knowing in the natural, as I was totally unaware of word curses, generational curses, and demons, etc., at that stage of my Christian walk. I said with great authority and fervor, "In the name of Jesus Christ, I break the power of that word curse spoken over Lisa, when she was a baby, by Dr. Vacarro that she would have rheumatoid arthritis when she grows up. I command that curse to be broken, and I speak to those knuckles and command them to be healed and normal by next Friday." I stepped back with wonder on my face, as did Lisa. We just looked at each other in amazement, not knowing what to think.

You see, in the natural, I did not even remember that diagnosis. Nor did I remember her pediatrician's name. Not only that, but I did not know anything about word curses. But the Holy Spirit did, and He took over and spoke through me. She came back the next Friday, and her knuckles were completely normal! To God be the glory!

What I learned from that incident with my daughter, Lisa, is that we do not have to automatically accept a medical diagnosis. We have the power, in the name of Jesus Christ who conquered all sickness and disease at the Cross of Calvary, to break and cast to the ground whatever diagnosis is given us. The name of Jesus is above every sickness and disease that the enemy of our souls can put upon us!

I have personally walked in divine health for many, many years as I immediately rebuke any symptoms the devil is trying to put upon me by saying something like, "No, you don't devil! I do not receive what you are trying to lay upon me. Take your ugly symptoms and depart from me." When I say "devil," I am addressing the demons assigned to me by the devil, who is Satan. There is one devil and many, many demons. Since their master is Satan, they know exactly what I am saying.

When colds and the flu are going around, and someone will say to me, "Oh, flu season is here. Everyone's getting sick," I will walk away and say, under my breath if I'm in public, "I cast those words to the ground! I am not catching any flu or getting sick!" You know something, it works! If you receive whatever the demons are trying to put upon you, such as a headache, cold, flu, it will come upon you full-blown! That's why the Word of God tells us to, "Resist the devil, and he will flee from," James 4:7 KJV.

It is also very important for us to take good care of our temples, our bodies, by eating healthy and staying away from junk food. God's best is for us to walk in divine health and not need healing. So in order to not impose upon the mercies of God, we need to take good care of our bodies by eating plenty of fresh fruits and vegetables and not abusing our bodies by putting garbage into them.

It's very common for us to see spirits of infirmity that have come down the family line, causing the same symptoms in generation after generation. Many times in the group deliverances that I hold, we see people who have not yet developed particular diseases be delivered of spirits of infirmity whose job function was to induce the disease at the opportune time.

I've cast out countless spirits of heart attack and premature death from Christians who've attended my deliverance sessions. Most of them had not seen the manifestation of those evil spirits in their bodies and lives. Those spirits will lay low, waiting for the opportune time to strike. Many times the demonic realm will set up situations that will be conducive to those spirits of infirmity and premature death. They may cause circumstances to be brought into the person's life whereby the person will be so stressed out or become hopeless that their body becomes weakened; then they can induce the infirmity for which they have been assigned to that person.

Also, if not dealt with, bitterness, anger, and the inability to forgive can affect the health of an individual. Many sicknesses are induced by emotional issues such as bitterness, anger, hatred, and inability to forgive. If a person holds on to any of these things for any extended period of time, spirits will enter in and reinforce that behavior. Once there are spirits behind these issues, they will start to affect the body in other ways, such as infirmity and sickness.

For those reading this book who have been severely abused as children by your parents, forgiveness may be something you're really struggling with. Or if you've been abused by a former spouse, you may be holding on to bitterness. Maybe if you understand what true forgiveness is, you'll be able to let go. In my twenty-seven-year walk with the Lord, I've heard some unscriptural things taught on the subject of forgiveness such as, we haven't truly forgiven if we don't want to go back into relationship with the person who has victimized us or hurt us. No wonder many find it impossible to forgive! If you've been victimized, whether by parents or former spouses, that kind of teaching would tie you back to the victimization, if the person has not repented and changed. That would be a very unhealthy thing to do!

Being a Christian doesn't mean being someone's punching bag or vessel for them to spew their poison into. Proper forgiveness doesn't mean forgetting, excusing, or accepting people or situations as they are. It is merely releasing those people who've hurt you and victimized you to God. He is the just and perfect judge and the avenger—not us. Forgiveness does not get the perpetrator off the hook; it only gets him out of our gut. It's been said that unwillingness to forgive is like you drinking poison and expecting the other person to die. Forgiveness is sometimes surrounded by needed boundaries. Forgiveness is not conceding to the offender or giving permission to the offender to hurt you again. Does that make it easier for you to forgive?

PRE-BIRTH EMOTIONAL DAMAGE

A study done on unborn children show us some very interesting things. A University of California professor, John Noonan, has been quoted as stating that by the tenth week of gestation, a baby's adrenal and thyroid glands are functioning. He sucks his thumb and responds to pain. He can kick, curl his toes, and turn his feet. His brain is formed much as it will be in adulthood, and his fingerprints already bear the pattern that is uniquely his. His heart has now been beating for seven weeks—pumping blood that he has made himself. So by the time the baby is two and a half months in the womb, he is experiencing life and recording those experiences in his brain.

How then, I ask, can we as a nation allow millions of these unborn babies (which we conveniently call "fetuses" to salve our conscience) to be murdered each year? Abortion is murder of an unborn baby. It's a modern day holocaust. The feminists have bumper stickers saying, "It's my body—freedom of choice," etc. But as we see from this study, once there's a baby inside the womb, it's no longer just the woman's body we're speaking of. There's another body there called a baby, not just a fetus. It is not my desire to cause wounds or bring condemnation to those in the church who have had abortions, but I remind each one of them of the forgiveness that is available. Studies show that as many as one in three women in churches today have gone through the horror of abortion. It is said that for each abortion there are two victims, the mother and the baby. Truly it is a no-win proposition and lie of the enemy!

In a book by Dr. Thomas Verny called *The Secret Life of the Unborn Child*, we see that the womb is the child's first world. How he experiences it creates personality and character predispositions. If the womb has been a warm, loving environment, the child is likely to expect the outside world to be the same. Since babies can hear and are completely aware of what is going on outside of the womb—such as strife or violence going on between mother and father—they will be experiencing the same emotions as the mother.

Unborn children are likely to pick up any rejection, anger, fear, dissatisfaction, or resentment that the mother is carrying and will interpret those emotions as directed toward themselves.

Other experts tell us that the mother's attitude toward her baby has the greatest single effect on how an infant turns out, and the quality of a woman's relationship with her husband rates second and has a decisive effect on the unborn child as well.

If the pregnancy was not wanted, the child will feel that rejection and a spirit of rejection will enter into the baby. In addition, a child whose mother feels rejected will likely feel rejected also. Children who are adopted will always have a stronghold of rejection operating in them, no matter how much they are wanted and loved by their adoptive parents. Although a baby cannot reason things out and come to logical conclusions, he knows things in his spirit.

Many times when we minister to people who have deep unworthiness, fear, or rejection, we will take them back to the time they were in their mother's womb. We will pray over that baby and release it from the rejection and fear, etc. Many have experienced great freedom with this type of ministry.

I had a woman call me from the east coast with this problem. She adopted a boy when he was just a baby. She and her husband had lavished this boy with as much love as a human can give to another. He was the most wanted child around. They did everything for him. When she called me, she proceeded to tell me that he'd always put up a wall around himself and acted sullen and resentful and basically unloved!

I then shared with her that his problem was a spirit of rejection that was operating in him. I told her that this is a heavy spirit that seems to operate in many adopted children, regardless of how much their adoptive parents love them. It is something they know when they are in their mother's womb. She was amazed at that revelation.

When I was young in the ministry of deliverance, I ministered to a great big hulk of a man who had a ponytail and tattoos all over his body. He was a man who had been serving and loving Jesus for many years but was struggling with issues that had never been addressed.

As I interviewed him, I found that he'd been adopted by a very loving couple. His birth mother, who he never knew, had shopped around for the best possible adoptive parents for him. He was given a very good life, but as an adult he went into rebellion. He had joined Hell's Angels motorcycle group, before he got saved.

When I told him that rebellion was the fruit and the root of that was rejection, he vehemently disagreed with me. He said he'd never felt rejection because his adoptive parents had been so loving. I asked him to humor me and let me call up a spirit of rejection before I went for rebellion.

Well, when I called up rejection, his entire body contorted, and that spirit was so strong that it shut down his vocal cords and wouldn't let him speak the renunciations. The spirit tried to throw him off the chair he was seated on. And he thought he didn't have rejection!

Most people who come in for deliverance and inner healing have roots of self-rejection and self-hatred; many times the problem lies in the knowledge they had before birth, while in the womb, that their parents did not want them. Other times the self-rejection and self-hatred comes from emotionally abusive parents or neglectful parents. But for those who received that message while in the womb, that message of rejection gets personalized, and they are born feeling unwanted.

Rejection of Sexuality

There is also the case of the mother who wants a boy child and the baby turns out to be a girl. That girl baby will sense in the womb that her sexuality is rejected and will consequently reject her own sexuality. She will most likely be a "tomboy" and never feel like she fits in with women.

Or the converse can be true. A mother wanting a girl and the baby is born a boy. Well, the message that baby received in the womb was that he was the wrong sex and this can lead to feminine mannerisms, etc. This was the case of a young man I ministered to a few months ago. His mother told me that when he was in the womb, she desperately wanted it to be a girl. As a result, she said that her son now shows effeminate tendencies.

When I ministered to him, I had his mother ask forgiveness for wanting a girl rather than a boy and had her affirm that he was exactly what God wanted him to be. I had him read Psalm 139:

For you created my inmost being; you knit me together in my mother's womb. I praise you because I am fearfully and wonderfully made; wonderful are your works, oh Lord. I know that full well. My frame was not hidden from you when I was made in the secret place. When I was woven together in the depths of the earth, your eyes saw my un-formed body. All the days ordained for me were written in your book before one of them came to be.

Psalm 139:13–16

This scripture shows us how God knew us before we were ever in our mother's womb and knows all that our days will hold before they ever come to be. What an awesome God we have!

God Doesn't Make Mistakes

It is important to come to the correct spiritual understanding that God created us as we are and each and every one of us is special to Him. To not accept the person we are and to dislike or even hate the body or personality he's given us is to imply that God made a mistake when creating us. God doesn't make mistakes. We are accepted in the beloved, and we are fearfully and wonderfully made in His image!

The only one who can heal us of our self-rejection and unworthiness and self-hatred is God. And, of course, one of the ways He does that is through the ministry of inner healing and deliverance.

Satan and his hordes of hell have been very effective in their strategy to mess people up in the self-image department. If he can keep us from knowing who we really are, who God created us to be, and keep us crippled emotionally, then he has suc-ceeded in keeping us from fulfilling our God-given destinies and purposes in the kingdom of God.

Our sense of personal worth should come from knowing who God says we are! We are children of God, created in His image! It's been said, "The more I become like Jesus, the more I become like me." In other words, the only way we "find ourselves" and can love and accept ourselves is to first find out who our Creator is. Then we find out who He created us to be. Unfortunately, most of us never get a real revelation of the love of God in our lives because we don't spend enough time with the Lord for Him to reveal these things to us. It's only through intimate time spent in prayer, in the Word, and worship that we can begin to know the Lord and He can begin to speak to us.

How can we fulfill the great commandment, "Love your neighbor as you love yourself," when we don't even love ourselves? Actually, the irony is most of us fulfill that commandment on a different level, the attitude being, "I hate me, and I hate you too!" We love the other guy with the same lack of love we feel for ourselves! How can we love others if we don't personally experience the love of God and then through that learn to love ourselves unconditionally?

No matter what our parents may have wanted or not wanted, we were planned and brought into being by the Almighty God, the Creator of the universe. Go back to the chapter on Emotional Inner Healing to remind yourself what God says about us. If you have a strong spirit of rejection or self-hate operating in you, this will probably not really penetrate into your heart. Once that spirit is cast out, then you can receive the reality of what God says about you and what His Word says about you. I know that from many years of experience in inner healing and deliverance. In fact, I have one specific incident in mind, which I believe will help you to understand this concept.

I was ministering to a young woman who had a deep and very real struggle with rejection brought in through dysfunctional parents who didn't care if she lived or died as she was growing up. I tried to tell her who she was according to God's Word, how special God had made her and how much He loved her. It just didn't register with her. I even tried sending the heavenly Father's love into her (which had always worked for others with similar issues), all to no avail. When I finally cast out the spirit of rejection, which was very strong and *then* sent into her the heavenly Father's love, she was visibly shaking. She told me afterwards that it felt like she'd just received a "heart hug." She was weeping with joy as she felt, for the first time in her life, real love.

Prophesy Fulfilled

For those reading this book who don't believe that the Word of God is true, every word *is* true, let me give you just one tiny example from the Bible. It may help you comprehend the awesomeness of the God who created us and the fact that he *knew* us before we were ever in our Mother's womb.

The book of 2 Chronicles ends with God's people, the Israelites, being taken into captivity by the Babylonians. This judgment against God's chosen people did not come without much warning. God is long-suffering and merciful. He always speaks in mercy and love first if we refuse, He then speaks in judgment.

He had warned Israel and Judah over and over again to turn from their wicked ways. It says in 2 Chronicles:

> The Lord, the God of their fathers, sent word to them through his messengers again and again, because he had pity on his people and on his dwelling place. But they mocked God's messengers, despised His words, and scoffed at His prophets until the wrath of the Lord was aroused against his people and there was no remedy. He brought up against them the king of the Babylonians—God handed all of them over to Nebuchadnezzar.
>
> 2 Chronicles 36:15 (NIV)

God had spoken through His prophet Jeremiah that the people would be in captivity for seventy years, which was fulfilled in 2 Chronicles, chapter 36. Then history tells us that after Nebuchadnezzar died in 562, because his successors were not strong, Babylon was overthrown by Persia in 539 with King Cyrus in charge, and that's where the next book of the Bible opens after 2 Chronicles, and it's called the book of Ezra. Cyrus was the Persian king who God used to make a proclamation that the Jews who had been in captivity for seventy years were now allowed to go back to Jerusalem in Judah and rebuild their city and their temple. This is all verified by history books, and that's why the Bible is the most accurate book ever written.

Cyrus and God's Nature

The thing that is so amazing, for those who don't believe that there is a God who is omniscient (possessing complete knowledge), is the fact that God named Cyrus 149 years before he was born. He is a God who knows our every thought. He knows the end from the beginning. He sees one hundred years from now as clearly as one hundred years ago. He is the Alpha and the Omega, the beginning and the end. Our God is an awesome God!

It was in Isaiah 44:28 and 45:1 that God spoke through the prophet Isaiah about Cyrus being the king who would be used to help the Jews return to Jerusalem. When God spoke these things through Isaiah, it was 149 years before Cyrus was born. So God knew that Cyrus would be given that name 149 years before he was even in his mother's womb. Tell me, does God know everything?

From that account we see two things about the nature of God:

1. He knows everything that is going to happen even before it happens. He knows what's going to happen one week from now, one month from now, and 200 years from now.

2. No matter what your parents tell you, you were not a mistake. God knew your name, just as He knew Cyrus's name, before you were even in your mother's womb. He has a destiny and purpose for you. The only way you will ever find satisfaction in this life is to serve God, and then He will help you to fulfill your destiny and purpose. We are all born for a purpose and don't have to live and die aimlessly. No matter what the circumstances of conception, you were chosen by God—even if it was rape or adultery. He had a plan for you. He didn't want the circumstances, but He wanted you!

Much of what happens grieves Him because He loves his creation, mankind. However because He has given man a free will, He will not interfere when someone chooses to sin and to walk in rebellion against Him. He may continue to send us signs pointing to the destruction that awaits should we continue down the wrong path. He is grieved by it because He knows the consequences of that sin and rebellion. He is grieved when He sees what mankind has done with the free will He has given them. There is always a price to pay for sin, and it's usually devastating.

THE POWER OF BLESSING

Another very vital part of Isaiah 61 Ministries is something the Lord showed me years ago, and whenever we do this it brings such great healing and freedom. What I'm speaking of is giving the Father's blessing to the people we minister to. Most who come in for ministry have been abused by their fathers or their mothers. But because God has created men to be the priests in the home, they have great power to either bless or curse their children.

I cannot state strongly enough the importance of the father's love in a child's life. We gain our self-identity from our fathers. That's just the order of things—how God created mankind.

Who does God call to raise up the children in the nurture and admonition of the Lord (Ephesians 6:4)? Fathers! If we have a poor self-image, it's usually due to poor fathering in our lives—an emotionally distant father or a father completely absent from the family.

In his book *Father Hunger*, Robert McGee states that the number one cause of criminal behavior is a poor father image. I agree with him to a certain extent, but there is also the factor of general curses being repeated, as I outlined earlier in this book. However, I do agree that fathers too often abdicate their roles of nurturing and loving their children. When the father doesn't do what he's supposed to do, there's an emptiness inside the children. When the father has failed to show love and acceptance, then the only other source of receiving that love and acceptance is found in Jesus Christ! If you are a father and have difficulty expressing true love and nurturing to your child, God the Father will give you that ability through His power.

Most of the people coming through the ministry have never received their father's blessing. So we stand in the gap for their earthly fathers who may have abused them or neglected them or been emotionally distant, and we ask forgiveness on behalf of their earthly father. Then we reverse the curses that came upon them because their fathers were not godly men. We use a wrap that we put around their shoulders and declare that it is the mantle of the father's love. Then we proclaim blessing over their lives. We declare over them that they "are blessed in the country, blessed in the city, that they are blessed when they come in and when they go out; that the blessings precede them and overflow them all the days of their lives," using some of the blessings from Deuteronomy chapter 28. We release them to be the men and women of God that they were created to be. There is always much weeping that goes on as we do this— great healing. And we know from great victory reports that there is a spiritual transaction that takes place in their lives.

EFFECTS OF CURSES

Let's look at some common evidences of a curse:

- Insanity, personality and emotional disturbances, depression and confusion.

- Infirmity, chronic sickness—i.e. heart problems, cancer, and other lingering ailments such as high blood sugar, diabetes, bone disease, and blood and respiratory diseases. Deuteronomy 28:21 mentions a pestilence that cleaves. The definition of pestilence is a contagious or infectious disease or something that is destructive. Infirmity that lingers and persists.

- Female problems, i.e. barrenness, problems with menstrual cycles such as severe cramps, tumors, and growth in the fallopian tubes and ovaries (many of these are caused by adultery in the bloodline or sexual perversion in the bloodline.) This curse affects the reproductive area of a woman's life.

- Divorce and strife in the family.

- Financial problems, despite faithfulness in tithing. When no matter how much you earn, you can never seem to get ahead. When even your "blessings" are cursed. In Haggai it says, "You have sown much and bring in little; you eat but you have not enough; you drink but are not filled with drink, you clothe you, but are not warm—he that earnest wages earnest wages to put it into a bag with holes" (Haggai 1:6, KJV). That's a financial curse in operation.

- Repeated accidents—either car accidents or injuries, broken bones, etc. This is usually due to occult sin in the bloodline or your own sin of the same, i.e. witchcraft, dabbling in tarot cards, horoscopes, and all the other things mentioned earlier in this book.

- Unnatural, premature, or violent deaths in the family. The Kennedy family is a prime example of this curse in operation. Even the secular media have called it "The Kennedy Curse." "But the wicked shall be cut off from the earth, and the transgressors shall be rooted out of it" (Proverbs 2:22, KJV). In Psalms it says, "... the seed of the wicked shall be cut off" (Psalm 37:28, KJV). It may not be anything you have done but rather what was done by one of your ancestors that has brought this curse into your life.

- Recurring job loss. You get to the pinnacle of success in your business endeavor and something happens, and everything comes tumbling down. You lose everything. This could be the result of either your past sin life or your ancestors' sins.

- Homelessness or housing problems. Foreclosures, fires, floods, vagabondism, lights, gas, telephone shut off, house burglarized, plumbing problems.

- Abuse: This includes mistreatment, which can be physical abuse, abusive marriages; sexual abuse including rape, incest, and verbal abuse; beatings, and robberies.

Curse of Automobile Accidents

Looking at repetitious accidents in our lives, have you ever noticed that when there is an accident in a certain location, i.e. stretch of freeway or certain corner of the street, that there will usually continue to be accidents in that same area? Have you ever wondered why?

This is yet another lesson on how the unseen spirit world operates. When there is an accident at a certain location, there is then a "curse of accidents" in operation in that spot. There are probably some powers of darkness stationed there to keep that curse in operation. I've seen that vividly displayed at least three times.

There was a stretch of Interstate 101 East in Phoenix that was having repeated accidents. I was not aware of that until I was driving with a friend one day, and she mentioned it. Apparently she had seen several accidents occur in the same stretch of freeway. As soon as I heard that, I broke the curse of automobile accidents in that spot and dismissed the powers of darkness from their assignments. I didn't hear of any more accidents in that spot.

I also noticed a bad accident one day at the intersection of 40th Street and Bell Road in Phoenix. Three days later as I was passing that same exact spot, there was another accident. Again I took the authority vested in me by the Lord Jesus Christ and broke that curse of accidents over that spot and have not seen another accident there as I drive by on a daily basis.

This is the type of thing we Christians should be doing on a consistent basis. We have power and authority over all the demonic realm, and we can stop the work of darkness wherever we see it. Let's not be unaware of the working of evil spirits behind most tragedies and disruptions in our world.

Far too many in the body of Christ are unwilling to engage in spiritual warfare and have adopted a passive attitude. They allow the enemy to walk all over them, taking every thing the enemy sends their way without resisting. *We* are supposed to be walking all over the enemy, not the other way around. Luke 10:19 instructs us to tread upon serpents and scorpions. How many Christians do you know who are doing just that?

If we are to be overcomers (and we are) we have to learn to go on the attack against the enemy. We give victory to the enemy when we remain passive and lose the battle by default. Even being on the defense is inadequate. Wars are never won by defensive measures.

Pleasure Cruise or Battle Ship?

Remember this dear reader, Christians walking in the authority Christ has given us are supposed to dictate the terms of the battle. We are supposed to engage in aggressive warfare; we are to persevere and prevail. That's the command given us in Matthew "…. The kingdom of heaven suffereth violence and the violent shall take it by force" (Matthew 11:12, KJV). A more modern day translation says this: "…The kingdom of heaven has been forcefully advancing, and forceful men lay hold of it" (Matthew 11:12, NIV). Both of these scriptures show us the reality of the difficulty and opposition of advancing the kingdom of heaven on this earth. And yet the American church seems to have the idea that the Christian life is some kind of a pleasure cruise. I don't see that anywhere in the Bible!

As believers, we have been given the mandate by Jesus Christ to take back what the enemy has stolen from our families, from our nation, from our culture. We are the enforcers of his victory at Calvary. We need to stop asking Jesus to do for us what He's already done. He said, "It is finished!" and now He is seated at the right hand of the Father, ever interceding on our behalf. When we get in our prayer closet and say something like, "Oh, Jesus, get the devil off my son or daughter," or

"Oh, Jesus, remove the sin from our society," He is sitting on the throne saying, "I've already given you the victory over all the powers of darkness, now *you* take that authority and forbid the enemy from having your children, etc." What we allow shall be allowed, what we do not allow cannot stand.

I pray that through the reading of this book that you've learned much about the invisible realm that is always at war over our lives and will have learned what it will take to "rebuild the old ruins" and "raise up the former desolations" and "repair the ruined cities (families), the desolations of many generations."

What I would encourage you to do as you finish reading this book is to sit down with your husband/wife and take spiritual inventory of your bloodline. What types of sins run in your mother's side of the bloodline, your father's side? What sins run in your husband's side of the bloodline—both his mother's side and father's side? What sins have you and your spouse committed? To free yourselves and your children and their descendants requires complete and total honesty. Satan loves "family secrets" so his demons can continue on in the bloodline. That's why he works so hard to put guilt, shame, and pride on people in the hopes that it'll keep them from exposing those sins and the demons can continue their ugly work unhindered.

As soon as you have your list prepared, you can go to work setting yourself and your descendants free from the grip of these ancestral sins by following the steps I have outlined for you.

If you have minor children still living with you, you can have them there with you as you and your husband start the process of breaking the curses of the past generations. If they're adult children and willing to gather with you for a family deliverance, it will be a great blessing to them and you. However, if they're unwilling, you can still break the curses off of them as you break them off yourselves and send the angels to get the demons out of them as you're getting them out of you.

GUIDELINE TO
BREAKING CURSES

The following are very basic instructions for a novice to use in breaking curses. What we do at Isaiah 61 Ministries is much more detailed and comprehensive, but this will suit your purposes.

First step: Bind (according to Matthew 18:18) the powers of the air over your place, and bind up the hordes of hell that are surrounding you. We are surrounded by unclean spirits at all times, but "there are more that are with us than those that are against us." The next step is to send confusion into the demonic realm. Then you need to loose the warring angels to war with you, and ask the Holy Spirit to flow through you and use you. If you don't instruct the angels, they won't assist. They will just stand by with their swords by their side. Oral Roberts says that when he had a heart attack and ended up in the hospital, he saw a huge angel at the foot of his bed and said, "Where were you when I needed you?" The angel replied, "I was with you, but you didn't tell me what to do."

Second step: Cover yourself, your loved ones, your possessions, your animals, everything that's near and dear to you in the blood of Jesus and bind and forbid retaliation, retribution, revenge, ambushment, and sabotage against yourselves, your loved ones, and your possessions.

Third step: Put warring angels to the right and left of everyone you're ministering deliverance to.

Fourth step: Forgive anyone who has ever hurt you. Earlier in this book I explained what true forgiveness is. You do not need to list what they did to you. God already knows that. Just list the people who you need to forgive, as unwillingness to forgive is a legal right for demons not to leave. The next step is asking forgiveness for your personal sins and the sins of your bloodline and then renouncing those sins.

What I have clients say is this: "Heavenly Father, in the name of Jesus and by the power of the Holy Spirit, I forgive the following people who've hurt me, and I release them to you to the best of my ability. I now forgive _____."

Then go on to say something like:

"Father, in the name of Jesus, I ask forgiveness for the following sins—both my own personal sins and those of my bloodline—on both my mother's side and father's side of the bloodline, and I renounce these sins and break their curses going all the way back to the beginning of my generational line on both sides of my bloodline and off of myself, my bloodline and all future generations. I now ask forgiveness for and renounce the following sins: (use the list of sins you have compiled)."

Note keeping is a very important part of the process. Date it and keep a running list of the curses broken and demons cast out so that the next time you resume the session, you'll be able to look at the previous notes and know where you left off. Work with "the sword of the Spirit,"—which, of course, is your Bible—in your hand to bring the demons up, and if you're having trouble, tell the angels of the Lord to bring up the demon.

Go over each curse one at a time, and after you have broken the curse, command every demon behind that curse to come out of you and your children and go directly to the pit. Forbid them from transferring to any living being, and tell the angels to take them directly to the pit. Then after the unclean spirit has left, I say, "I shut the door to lust, or whatever other unclean spirit, and I seal every door with the blood of Jesus." If a demon takes over the person and starts to speak through the person, do what I instructed earlier in this book. Have them renounce their claim to the person, their bloodline, and all future generations, etc.

It is a time-consuming process, and you cannot just command all of the demons behind those curses to come out at once—it just doesn't work that way. You deal with one at a time. You can do it bit by bit. Take one day a week for this process of deliverance. It may take you a month, but it will be well worth it. Remember when God sent Israel in to possess the promised land, they didn't destroy their enemies all at once, it was bit by bit.

There are various demonic manifestations when the demon is cast out of the person. It can be coughing, sneezing, belching, weeping, yawning, screaming or retching. Sometimes the person will just feel pain in his body as the demon exits, or their body will become flushed. I've had people tell me they felt like they were in a sauna as the demons exited. Everyone will have different manifestations. Sometimes the demons leaving will make the person's entire body shake. But usually the demons will come out on the breath and exit out of the mouth. Some people have told me they would feel the demons exiting out of their ears or the top of their head. Some people have demons exit through mucus in their noses.

As the demons are leaving, be either praying quietly in the Spirit or saying the name of Jesus over and over again—they hate the name of Jesus. However, the people receiving deliverance should not be praying and saying the name of Jesus, as demons will usually exit through the lips, on our breath, and they will not cross lips praising the Lord. They will go right back down again. Sometimes you have to affirm that the person's body is a temple of the Holy Spirit. The demons are trespassers in the temple of God, and they must leave.

Always remember this: Demons know authority. They do not respond to screaming and shouting—you'll just wear yourself out. I am just giving you the basics here. We are right now in the process of bringing deliverance conferences to the churches to educate the body of Christ on the subject of deliverance. It is also to get the body of Christ set free so that they can be all that God created them to be and do His work.

After you have finished the deliverance, say, "Holy Spirit, go into (the person who's been delivered) _____ with peace, love, joy, and restoration."

Then have the angels cleanse your home and property, and tell them that no demons are allowed to linger on your property. Cover yourselves, your loved ones, your possessions, your animals, and your health with the Blood of Jesus. Bind and forbid any retaliation, retribution, revenge, ambushment, and sabotage against yourselves, your loved ones, and possessions. Last but not least, give the glory to the Lord for what He has done. Praise Him for the wonderful gift of deliverance!

APPENDIX A

Prayer of Release for Freemasons and Their Descendants

If you were once a Mason or are a descendant of a Mason, we recommend that you pray through the following prayer from your heart. Don't be like the Masons who are given their obligations and oaths one line at a time and without prior knowledge of the requirements. Please read it through first so you know what is involved. It is best to pray this aloud with a Christian witness or counselor present. We suggest a brief pause following each paragraph to allow the Holy Spirit to show any additional issues which may require attention.

Father God, creator of heaven and earth, I come to you in the name of Jesus Christ, your Son. I come as a sinner seeking forgiveness and cleansing from all sins committed against you and others made in your image. I honor my earthly father and mother and all of my ancestors of flesh and blood and of the spirit by adoption and godparents, but utterly turn away from and renounce all their sins. I forgive all my ancestors for the effects of their sins on my children and me. I confess and renounce all of my own sins. I renounce and rebuke Satan and every spiritual power of his affecting my family and me.

I renounce and forsake all involvement in Freemasonry or any other lodge or craft by my ancestors and myself. I renounce witchcraft, the principal spirit behind Freemasonry, and I renounce Baphomet, the Spirit of Antichrist, and the curse of the Luciferian doctrine. I renounce the idolatry, blasphemy, secrecy, and deception of Masonry at every level. I specifically renounce the insecurity, the love of position and power, the love of money, avarice or greed, and the pride that would have led my ancestors into Masonry. I renounce all the fears that held them in Masonry, especially the fears of death, fears of men, and fears of trusting, in the name of Jesus Christ.

I renounce every position held in the lodge by any of my ancestors, including, "Tyler," "Master," "Worshipful Master," or any other. I renounce the calling of any man "Master," for Jesus Christ is my only master and Lord, and He forbids any-one else having that title. I renounce the entrapping of others into Masonry and observing the helplessness of others during the rituals. I renounce the effects of Masonry passed on to me through any female ancestor who felt distrusted and rejected by her husband as he entered and attended any lodge and refused to tell her of his secret activities.

First Degree

I renounce the oaths taken and the curses involved in the First or Entered Apprentice degree, especially their effects on the throat and tongue. I renounce the hoodwink, the blindfold, and its effects on emotions and eyes, including all confusion, fear of the dark, fear of the light, and fear of sudden noises. I renounce the secret word, *boaz*, and all it means. I renounce the mixing and mingling of truth and error, and the blasphemy of this degree of Masonry. I renounce the noose around the neck, the fear of choking, and also every spirit causing asthma, hay fever, emphysema, or any other breathing difficulty. I renounce the compass point, sword, or spear held against the breast, the fear of death by stabbing pain, and the fear of heart attack from this degree. In the name of Jesus Christ I now pray for healing of throat, vocal cords, nasal passages, sinus, bronchial tubes, etc., for healing of the speech area, and the release of the Word of God to me and through me and my family.

Second Degree

I renounce the oaths taken and the curses involved in the second or Fellow Craft degree of Masonry, especially the curses on the heart and chest. I renounce the secret words *jachin* and *shibboleth* and all that these mean. I cut off emotional hardness, apathy, indifference, unbelief, and deep anger from my family and me. In the name of Jesus Christ I pray for the healing of the chest, lung, and heart area and also for the healing of my emotions. I ask to be made sensitive to the Holy Spirit of God.

Third Degree

I renounce the oaths taken and the curses involved in the third or Master Mason degree, especially the curses on the stomach and womb area. I renounce the secret words *maha bone, machaben, machbinna, tubal cain,* and all that they mean. I renounce the spirit of death from the blows to the head enacted as ritual murder, the fear of death, false martyrdom, and fear of violent gang attack, assault, or rape, and the helplessness of this degree. I renounce the falling into the coffin or stretcher involved in the ritual of murder.

I renounce the false resurrection of this degree, because only Jesus Christ is the resurrection and the life! I also renounce the blasphemous kissing of the Bible on a witchcraft oath. I cut off all spirits of death, witchcraft, and deception, and in the name of Jesus Christ I pray for the healing of the stomach, gall bladder, womb, liver, and any other organs of my body affected by Masonry. I ask for a release of compassion and understanding for my family and me.

Holy Royal Arch Degree

I renounce and forsake the oaths taken and the curses involved in the Holy Royal Arch Degree of Masonry, especially the oath regarding the removal of the head from the body and the exposing of the brains to the hot sun. I renounce the Mark Lodge, and the mark in the form of squares and angles which marks the person for life. I also reject the jewel or talisman, which may have been made from this mark sign and worn at lodge meetings. I renounce the false secret name of God, Jahbulon, and the password, ammi ruhamah, and all they mean. I renounce the false communion or Eucharist taken in this degree, and all the mockery, skepticism, and unbelief about the redemptive work of Jesus Christ on the cross of Calvary. I cutoff all these curses and their effects on my family and me in the name of Jesus Christ. I pray for healing of the brain, the mind, etc.

Eighteenth Degree

I renounce the oaths taken and the curses involved in the eighteenth degree of Masonry, the Most Wise Sovereign Knight of the Pelican and the Eagle and Sovereign Prince Rose Croix of Heredom. I renounce and reject the Pelican witchcraft spirit, as well as the occult influence of the Rosicrucian's and the Kabala in this degree. I renounce the claim that the death of Jesus Christ was a "dire calamity," and also the deliberate mockery and twisting of the Christian doctrine of the atonement. I renounce the blasphemy and rejection of the deity of Jesus Christ, and the secret words *igne natura renovatur integra* and its burning. I renounce the mockery of the communion taken in this degree, including a biscuit, salt, and white wine.

Thirtieth Degree

I renounce the oaths taken and the curses involved in the thirtieth degree of Masonry, the Grand Knight Kadosh and Knight of the Black and White Eagle. I renounce the password, *stibium alkabar*, and all it means.

Thirty-first Degree

I renounce the oaths taken and the curses involved in the thirty-first degree of Masonry, the Grand Inspector Inquisitor Commander. I renounce all the gods and goddesses of Egypt, which are honored in this degree, including Anubis, with the ram's head; Osiris, the Sun god; Isis, the sister and wife of Osiris; and also the moon goddess. I renounce the soul of Cheres, the false symbol of immortality, the chamber of the dead, and the false teaching of reincarnation.

Thirty-second Degree

I renounce the oaths taken and the curses involved in the thirty-second degree of Masonry, the Sublime Prince of the Royal Secret. I renounce Masonry's false Trinitarian deity AUM, and its parts: Brahma, the creator; Vishnu, the preserver; and Shiva, the destroyer. I renounce the deity of Ahura-Mazda, the claimed spirit or source of all light, and the worship with fire, which is an abomination to God. Also the drinking from a human skull in many rites.

York Rite

I renounce the oaths taken and the curses involved in the York Rite of Freemasonry, including Mark Master, Past Master, Most Excellent Master, Royal Master, Select Master, Super Excellent Master, the Orders of the Red Cross, the Knights of Malta, and the Knights Templar degrees. I renounce the secret words of *joppa*, *keb raioth*, and *maher-shalal-hash-baz*. I renounce the vows taken on a human skull, the crossed swords, and the curse and death wish of Judas of having the head cut off and placed on top of a church spire. I renounce the unholy communion and especially of drinking from a human skull in many rites.

Shriners

I renounce the oaths taken and the curses and penalties involved in the Ancient Arabic Order of the Nobles of the Mystic Shrine. I renounce the piercing of the eyeballs with a three-edged blade, the flaying of the feet, the madness, and the worship of the false god Allah as the god of our fathers. I renounce the hoodwink, the mock hanging, the mock beheading, the mock drinking of the blood of the victim, the mock dog urinating on the initiate, and the offering of urine as a commemoration.

Thirty-third Degree

I renounce the oaths taken and the curses involved in the thirty-third degree of Masonry, the Grand Sovereign Inspector General. I renounce and forsake the declaration that Lucifer is God. I renounce the cable-tow around the neck. I renounce the death wish that the wine drunk from a human skull should turn to poison and the skeleton whose cold arms are invited if the oath of this degree is violated. I renounce the three infamous assassins of their grandmaster, law, property, religion, and the greed and witchcraft involved in the attempt to manipulate and control the rest of mankind.

All Other Degrees

I renounce all the other oaths taken, the rituals of every other degree, and the curses involved. I renounce all other lodges and secret societies such as Prince Hall Freemasonry, Mormonism, and the Order of Amaranth, Odd fellows, Buffalos, Druids, Foresters, Orange, Elks, Moose and Eagles Lodges, the Ku Klux Klan, the Grange, the Woodmen of the World, Riders of the Red Robe, the Knights of Pythias, the Mystic Order of the Veiled Prophets of the Enchanted Realm, the women's Orders of the Eastern Star, and of the White Shrine of Jerusalem, the girls' order of the Daughters of the Eastern Star, the International Orders of Job's Daughters, and of the Rainbow, and the boys' Order of De Molay, and their effects on all my family and me.

Order of the Eastern Star

I renounce the ancient pagan teaching and symbolism of the First Tracing Board, the Second Tracing Board, and the Third Tracing Board used in the ritual of the Blue Lodge. I renounce the pagan ritual of the "Point within a Circle" with all its bondages and phallus worship. I renounce the occult mysticism of the black and white mosaic checkered floor with the tessellated border and five-pointed blazing star. I renounce the symbol *G* and its veiled pagan symbolism and bondages. I renounce and utterly forsake the Great Architect of the universe, who is revealed in the higher degrees as Lucifer, and his false claim to be the universal fatherhood of God. I also renounce the false claim that Lucifer is the Morning Star and Shining One, and I declare that Jesus Christ is the Bright and Morning Star of Revelation 22:16.

I renounce the "All-Seeing Third Eye" of Freemasonry or horns in the forehead and its pagan and occult symbolism. I renounce all false communions taken, all mockery of the redemptive work of Jesus Christ on the cross of Calvary, all unbelief, confusion and depression, and all worship of Lucifer as God. I renounce and forsake the lie of Freemasonry that man is not sinful but merely imperfect and so can redeem himself through good works. I rejoice that the Bible states that I cannot do a single thing to earn my salvation, but I can only be saved by grace through faith in Jesus Christ and what He accomplished on the Cross of Calvary.

I renounce all fear of insanity, anguish, death wishes, suicide, and death in the name of Jesus Christ. Death was conquered by Jesus Christ, and He alone holds the keys of death and hell. I rejoice that He holds my life in His hands now. He came to give me life abundantly and eternally, and I believe His promises.

I renounce all anger, hatred, murderous thoughts, revenge, retaliation, spiritual apathy, false religion, all unbelief, especially unbelief in the Holy Bible as God's Word, and all compromise of God's Word. I renounce all spiritual searching into false religions and all striving to please God. I rest in the knowledge that I have found my Lord and Savior Jesus Christ and that He has found me.

I will burn all objects in my possession which connect me with all lodges and occult organizations, including Masonry, witchcraft, and Mormonism; and all regalia, aprons, books of rituals, rings, and other jewelry. I renounce the effects these or other objects of Masonry, such as the compass, the square, the noose, or the blindfold have had on me or my family, in Jesus's name.

All participants should now be invited to sincerely carry out the following:

1. *Symbolically remove the blindfold (hoodwink) and give it to the Lord for disposal.*

2. *In the same way, symbolically remove the veil of mourning.*

3. *Symbolically cut and remove the noose from around the neck, gather it up with the cable-tow running down the body and give it all to the Lord far His disposal.*

4. *Renounce the false Freemasonry marriage covenant, removing from the fourth finger of the right hand the ring of this false marriage covenant, giving it to the Lord to dispose of it.*

5. *Symbolically remove the chains and bandages of Freemasonry from your body.*

6. *Symbolically remove all Freemasonry regalia and armor, especially the Apron.*

7. *Invite participants to repent of and seek forgiveness for having walked on all unholy ground, including Freemasonry lodges and temples, including any Mormon or other occult Masonic organizations.*

8. *Symbolically remove the ball and chain from the ankles.*

9. *Proclaim that Satan and his demons no longer have any legal rights to mislead and manipulate the persons seeking help.*

Holy Spirit, I ask that you show me anything else that I need to do or to pray so that my family and I may be totally free from the consequences of the sins of Masonry, witchcraft, Mormonism, and paganism.

(Pause, while listening to God, and pray as the Holy Spirit leads you.)

Now dear Father God, I ask humbly for the blood of Jesus Christ, your Son, to cleanse me from all these sins I have confessed and renounced, to cleanse my spirit, my soul my mind, my emotions, and every part of my body that has been affected by these sins, in Jesus's name!

I renounce every evil spirit associated with Masonry and witchcraft and all other sins, and I command in the name of Jesus Christ for Satan and every evil spirit to be bound and to leave me now, touching or harming no one, and to go to the pit, never to return to me or my family. I call on the name of the Lord Jesus to be delivered of every spirit of sickness, infirmity, curse, affliction, addiction, disease, or allergy associated with these sins I have confessed and renounced. I surrender to God's Holy Spirit and to no other spirit all the places in my life where these sins have been. I ask you Lord to baptize me in your Holy Spirit now according to the promises in your Word. I take to myself the whole armor of God in accordance with Ephesians chapter 6 and rejoice in its protection as Jesus surrounds me and fills me with His Holy Spirit. I enthrone you, Lord Jesus, in my heart, for you are my Lord and my Savior, the source of eternal life. Thank you, Father God, for your mercy, your forgiveness, and your love, in the name of Jesus Christ. Amen.

APPENDIX B

Daily Warfare Prayer Covering

This is also a very good daily prayer covering. I have had many people tell me that when they remember to use the prayer covering in the morning before they start their day that everything goes well, and when they forget, the converse is true. This is just a suggestion for your warfare—you can add those things that seem to attack you on a consistent basis and eliminate those things that don't pertain to your family when you do the binding. But we need to be on the offensive against the enemy on a daily basis. Satan is ever plotting to bring you and your loved ones down. We need to get him on the run. He and his hordes of hell should tremble when you awake in the morning, knowing you're a threat to his kingdom and his plans and strategies.

Daily Warfare Prayer Covering

In the name of Jesus and by the power of the Holy Spirit, according to Matthew 18:18, I bind, rebuke, and bring to no effect over myself, my spouse, and children (list all by name), the following spirits and their outworking in our lives:

All division, discord, disunity, strife, anger, wrath, murder, criticism, condemnation, pride, envy, jealousy, gossip, slander, evil speaking, complaining, lying, false teaching, false gifts, false manifestations, lying signs, wonders, poverty, fear of lack, fear spirits, murmuring spirits, complaining spirits, hindering spirits, retaliatory spirits, deceiving spirits, religious spirits, occult spirits, witchcraft spirits, and antichrist spirits. All foolishness, seduction, immorality, unbelief, idolatry, ignorance, accidents, confusion, infirmity, accusation, fraud, sickness, judgment, and superstition. I bind, rebuke, and bring to no effect all addiction to alcohol , (or whatever the addictions may be), all bondage, death, hell, all destruction, self-destruction, stubbornness, all rebellion, all spiritual, mental and emotional oppressions, all torment, etc. (Tailor the binding to whatever problems are prevalent in your loved ones' lives). I bind all of hell's plans for our lives this day and loose all of our heavenly Father's plans into our lives this day.

I loose God's plans, God's will, into my life and my loved ones' lives this day. I loose peace, love, and joy into our lives this day. I oppose and thwart Satan's plans against us this day and night.

I break all curses that have been spoken against me and my loved ones—all witchcraft curses and word curses. I bind all spoken judgments made against us and judgments we have made against other. I bind the power of negative words from others, and I bind and render useless all prayers not inspired by the Holy Spirit, whether psychic, soul force, witchcraft, or counterfeit tongues that have been prayed against us.

I declare that my loved ones and I are God's children. I resist the devil for each one of us. No weapon formed against us shall prosper. I put the full armor of God on each one of us, then proceed to put on the full armor, the breastplate of righteousness, for this day. I take authority over this day in Jesus's name. Let it be prosperous for us. Lord let us walk in your love, in your blessings, with the host of heaven ministering to us and protecting us from all the powers of darkness.

Holy Spirit, lead and guide us today. Help us to discern between the righteous and the wicked. I call forth divine appointments, God-ordained encounters and ministry positions. If you have unmarried children: I call forth God-ordained marriages for _____. Anoint us for all you've called us to do.

I take authority over Satan and his demons and those people that are influenced by Satan and his demons. I declare that Satan is under my feet throughout this day and night.

My loved ones and I are the righteousness of God in Christ Jesus. We are God's property. Satan, you are bound from our minds, our bodies, our homes, and our finances. I declare that we are healed and whole, that we flourish, are long-lived, stable, durable, incorruptible, fruitful, virtuous, and full of peace, patience, and love. I declare that I and my loved ones will fulfill our God-appointed destinies. Whatever we set our hands to shall prosper, for God supplies all of our needs. I have all authority over Satan, his demons, and beasts of the field. I forbid Satan, his demons, and beasts of the field from coming against myself and my loved ones throughout this day and night.

I claim a hedge of protection around my loved and myself ones throughout this day and night. I ask you, Father, in the name of Jesus, to dispatch angels to surround us. Put them throughout our homes, our cars, souls, bodies, and everywhere our feet set this day. I ask for angels to protect our home from any intrusion and to protect my loved ones and me from any harmful demonic attack—physical or mental.

Standing Against Witchcraft

Also we need to be returning any witchcraft that is being sent to us at the end of every day. Whether you know it or not, Christians are always being targeted by those in witchcraft and the occult. One of the first things I do when I hold a group deliverance is to break all witchcraft off of everyone attending and reverse the curses, according to Psalm 109:17. When I do that, almost the entire audience starts to cough and gag as those witchcraft curses come out of them.

Now, I know that there will be those reading this book who will think that as Christians we should not be sending back curses, that we should be praying for these people. For those of you who are in that category, remember this is warfare. We have a very real enemy who is using people who've sold themselves out to him, and their aim is to destroy Christians. The demonic world hates Christians! When we were fighting the Nazis in WWII, do you think it would have been appropriate for the Allied Forces to embrace the Nazis? I don't think so. War is war—whether natural or spiritual. Besides, we did not initiate those curses; we are simply sending them back in the hope that they will realize that our God is greater than their god and will eventually give up their evil ways.

All too often the American church sends missionaries into third world countries where witchcraft, voodoo, sorcery, and every form of spirituality is being practiced without teaching the missionaries how to protect themselves and break the witchcraft and whatever else is sent to them. The consequence of that is that many end up sick and die from unexplainable causes, because no one knows how to break those curses, hexes, vexes, and spells that have been put on them.

Remember, dear reader, Satanists, witches, wizards, and warlocks are constantly doing unholy fasts against Christians. We have to stop "burying our heads in the sand" and begin to recognize the source of many of our problems and illnesses. I have been walking in divine health for years now because at the end of every day, I send back any witchcraft that was sent to me that day. I can oftentimes feel things lifting off of my body! The warfare prayer for sending back curses is the following (and remember you need to do it with authority and faith):

> I loose warring angels to war with me, and I ask you Holy Spirit to war through me. Right now, in the name of Jesus and by the power of the Holy Spirit, I break the power of all witchcraft that has been sent to me through this day and night. I send it back to the senders according to Psalm 109:17. I break the power of all voodoo, sorcery, shamanism, Satanism, hexes, vexes, spells, unholy fasts, and blood sacrifices that have been sent to me, and I command every unclean spirit behind that to go back to the sender according to Psalm 109:17.

I then command my bedroom to be cleansed of all demons, dark angels, unclean spirits, and then I send the Blood of Jesus over the floors, the walls, the ceilings, every item in my room, and I seal off the room with the blood of Jesus. I then loose the warring angels to fill up my bedroom to prevent demonic activity in the night, and the ministering spirits to minister deep sound sleep to me.

I then sleep uninterrupted sleep, without attack in the night season. Prior to learning to do this type of spiritual warfare, I was being attacked every night, preventing me from getting sound sleep, and many times would awaken with some sort of sickness or infirmity that would be laid on me as I slept. That does not happen any more!

My prayer is that through the reading of this book, you have come to the knowledge of the source of many of your problems, and you now will have the understanding of how to "lay the axe" to the root of those problems. May this book cause God's army to arise and do exploits in His name.

APPENDIX C

Dream Covering

One of the most common ways Gods speaks to us is through dreams. It would only make sense that God would speak to us while we are sleeping since a full one-third of our lives are spent sleeping! While it is necessary to say that certainly not all dreams are spiritual, many dreams we do dismiss or write off are very important messages from God. I've had many who've told me when they started covering their dream state and sleep state, they'd get dreams from the Lord.

We see God speaking to His people in dreams throughout the Old Testament and New Testament. It is one of His ways of leading, guiding, and instructing us in the way we should go. He is very pleased when we come to Him as our source of leading, rather than to human resources. He knows "the end from the beginning" and can give you the best possible solution to whatever problem you're praying about. He sees the whole picture and also knows things going on in whatever situation we're concerned about. He knows the hearts of the people involved. While in a multitude of counselors there is wisdom, it is also wisdom to go to the Greatest Counselor, the Holy Spirit. The

Holy Spirit will never mislead us! We see God speaking to his people in dreams in Genesis chapters 20, 26, 28, 31, 37, 40, 41, and 46, just to name a few. I encourage you to do a thorough biblical study to see from Genesis to Revelation just how often God speaks to His people in dreams.

Although you can receive biblical advice from well-meaning people, they still don't know everything involved in your situation. The Holy Spirit does. Many times He tries speaking to us in dreams regarding whatever is troubling us, but due to ignorance, we throw out the dream like junk mail.

The only book on dreams that I recommend is Ira Milligan's *Understanding The Dreams You Dream* and the follow up book *Every Dreamer's Handbook.*

The Holy Spirit has had me compile a Dream Covering Prayer that has helped multitudes of people begin to hear from God in the night. I'm told over and over again by those who never got dreams, that every time they pray the dream covering, they get a dream from God. It is very exciting to be able to get personal instruction from God concerning different issues in our lives.

Pray along these lines:

> According to Matthew 18:18, I bind away from myself any spirit that is not the Spirit of the Lord—all unclean spirits and demons—and I command them to leave me now. I bind away from myself all dream-stealing and dream-blocking demons, all soulish dreams, all counterfeit dreams, and all demonic dreams. I bind any demons that would pollute spiritual dreams and visions, and I command them to leave me now. I bind up the closed heavens over me now, and I command the heavens to be opened with angels ascending and descending from the throne of God with dreams, instruction, leading, guidance, and direction. I cover my dream state and sleep state in the blood

of Jesus. I put on the helmet of salvation, and I bind my dreams and my sleep to the Lord Jesus Christ.

I now take authority over this room and command it to be cleansed of all unclean spirits, anything that is not of God. Angels of God, bind these things up now and send them to the pit.

Then I send the blood of Jesus over the floors, the walls, the ceiling and I seal off the opening of this bedroom with the Blood of Jesus. I put a wall of fire around my bed and a canopy of fire over that. I assign warring angels to stand guard over me and protect me from any nighttime attacks. I loose the warrior angels to fill up my room to prevent any demonic activity in the night. I assign ministering spirits to bring me in remembrance of every detail of the dreams I dream.

Having done that, spend time with the Holy Spirit telling him what your concerns are and what you need answers to.

Then bring before the Lord the following by saying something like:

Lord your Word says in Jeremiah 33:3, "When I call upon you, you will answer me. You will show me great and mighty things, things I have not known." Job 33:14, "God speaketh once, yea, twice, in a dream, in a vision, when deep sleep falleth upon men and He sealeth instruction to their hearts." Psalm 32:8, "I will instruct you and teach you in the way that you should go. I will counsel you and keep my eyes on you." Psalm 16:7, "I will praise the Lord who counsels me; even at night my heart instructs me."

If you leave the bedroom after having cleansed yourself of unclean spirits, when you return, command any unclean spirits that followed you back into your room to leave you. Unseal the opening of the room just so they can be escorted out and then seal it again, so as to not get demonic interference in your sleep.

When trying to interpret the dreams that God gives you: Go into the dream book *Understanding the Dreams you Dream*, by Ira Milligan, and get all the explanation of the symbolism. God speaks in mysteries. Keep a dream journal by your bedside and write the dream down as soon as you awaken so you don't forget the details. Then when you get into your prayer time, pray over the dream in the spirit and ask the Holy Spirit to release the Daniel anointing and Joseph anointing for interpretation of dreams. Many times God will give you prophetic dreams that are for the future.

Problems with Insomnia:

> I bind, according to Matthew 18:18, Insomnia, fear of insomnia, wakefulness, restlessness, interrupted sleep, sleeplessness. I bind all evil nighttime creatures. I cancel every spiritual problem associated with the hours of 9:00 p.m. and 9:00 a.m., or whatever time you go to sleep and awaken. I neutralize all nighttime attacks, and I bind all nighttime harassment and nighttime torment.

Then quote Proverbs 3:24, "When I lie down, I will not be afraid. When I lie down, my sleep will be sweet," and Psalm 127:2, "Thank you, Lord, that you give your beloved sleep."

BIBLIOGRAPHY

Billheimer, Paul, *Destined To Overcome*, 1st Ed. Bethany House Publishers, 1982

Billheimer, Paul, *Destined For The Throne*, 2nd Ed. Bethany House Publishers, 1996

Grant, Jeffrey, *Unveiling the Mysteries Of The Bible*, 2nd Ed. Harmony Printing, Ltd. 2002

Hegstrom, Paul, *Broken Children, Grown-Up Pain*, 1st Ed. Beacon Press Of Kansas City,2001

Horrobin, Peter, *Healing Through Deliverance*, 2nd Ed. Sovereign World Ltd. 1994

Huch, Larry, *Free At Last*, 2nd Ed. Albury Publishing, 2000

Ing, Richard, *Spiritual Warfare*, 1st Ed. Whitaker House, 1996

Malone, Henry, Shadow Boxing, 2nd Ed. Vision Life Publication, 2001

Murphy, Ed, Dr. *The Handbook of Spiritual Warfare*, 3rd Ed. Thomas Nelson Publishers, 2003

Prince, Derek, *They Shall Expel Demons*, 13 Ed. Chosen Books, 2005

Seamands, David, *Healing For Damaged Emotions*, 1st Ed. Scripture Press Publishers, 1981

Stevens, Selwyn, *Unmasking Freemasonry: Removing the Hoodwink*, Lst Ed. Jubilee Publishers, 1999

Tetlow, Oakland, Myers, *Queen Of All*, Eternal Productions, 1st Ed. 2006

Verny, Thomas, Md, With John Kelly, *The Secret Life of the Unborn Child*, Lst Ed Dell Books, 1982

Whiston, William, *the Works Of Josephus*, 16 Ed. Hendrickson Publishers, Inc. 2001

Made in the USA
San Bernardino, CA
14 March 2017